TIMED READINGS

in Literature

BOOK NINE

Edward Spargo, Editor

Selections & Questions
for this Edition:
Henry Billings
Melissa Billings

Fifty 400-Word Passages
with Questions for
Building Reading Speed

Jamestown Publishers

Titles in This Series
Timed Readings, Third Edition
Timed Readings in Literature

Teaching Notes are available for this text and
will be sent to the instructor. Please write on
school stationery; tell us what grade
you teach and identify the text.

Timed Readings in Literature

Catalog No. 919

Cover and text design by Deborah Hulsey Christie

Printed in the United States HS

4 5 6 7 8 9 10 11 12 13 14   <u>021</u>   10 09 08 07 06 05 04 03 02 01

ISBN: 0-89061-522-5

Contents

Introduction to the Student

These *Timed Readings in Literature* are designed to help you become a faster and better reader. As you progress through the book, you will find yourself growing in reading speed and comprehension. You will be challenged to increase your reading rate while maintaining a high level of comprehension.

Reading, like most things, improves with practice. If you practice improving your reading speed, you will improve. As you will see, the rewards of improved reading speed will be well worth your time and effort.

Why Read Faster?

The quick and simple answer is that faster readers are better readers. Does this statement surprise you? You might think that fast readers would miss something and their comprehension might suffer. This is not true, for two reasons:

1. Faster readers comprehend faster. When you read faster, the writer's message is coming to you faster and makes sense sooner. Ideas are interconnected. The writer's thoughts are all tied together, each one leading to the next. The more quickly you can see how ideas are related to each other, the more quickly you can comprehend the meaning of what you are reading.

2. Faster readers concentrate better. Concentration is essential for comprehension. If your mind is wandering you can't understand what you are reading. A lack of concentration causes you to re-read, sometimes over and over, in order to comprehend. Faster readers concentrate better because there's less time for distractions to interfere. Comprehension, in turn, contributes to concentration. If you are concentrating and comprehending, you will not become distracted.

Want to Read More?

Do you wish that you could read more? (or, at least, would you like to do your required reading in less time?) Faster reading will help.

The illustration on the next page shows the number of books someone might read over a period of ten years. Let's see what faster reading could

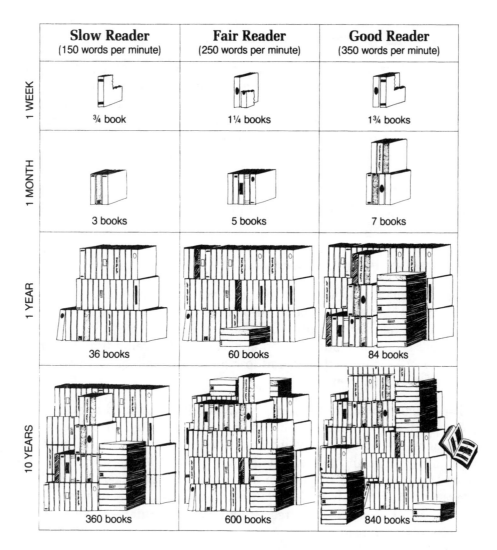

	Slow Reader (150 words per minute)	Fair Reader (250 words per minute)	Good Reader (350 words per minute)
1 WEEK	¾ book	1¼ books	1¾ books
1 MONTH	3 books	5 books	7 books
1 YEAR	36 books	60 books	84 books
10 YEARS	360 books	600 books	840 books

do for you. Look at the stack of books read by a slow reader and the stack read by a good reader. (We show a speed of 350 words a minute for our "good" reader, but many fast readers can more than double that speed.) Let's say, however, that you are now reading at a rate of 150 words a minute. The illustration shows you reading 36 books a year. By increasing your reading speed to 250 words a minute, you could increase the number of books to 60 a year.

We have arrived at these numbers by assuming that the readers in our illustration read for one hour a day, six days a week, and that an average book is about 72,000 words long. Many people do not read that much, but they might if they could learn to read better and faster.

Faster reading doesn't *take* time, it *saves* time!

Acquisitional *vs.* Recreational Reading

Timed Readings in Literature gives practice in a certain kind of reading: recreational reading. Recreational reading of novels and short stories is different from the kind of reading you must employ with textbooks. You read a textbook to *acquire* facts and information. That is acquisitional reading, reading that is careful and deliberate—you cannot afford to miss something you may be quizzed on later. Acquisitional reading speed must be slower than recreational reading speed.

The practice you will be doing in this book will help you develop a high reading speed suitable for literature.

Why Practice on Literature?

If acquisitional reading is so useful and important for students, why should you spend valuable class time learning to read literature faster? Shouldn't you be learning to read textbooks faster and better? Believe it or not, you are! That's right: the reading speed and skills you develop from this book will transfer to your textbooks and to other study reading. Here are some of the ways this happens.

1. The practice effect. In the dictionary, *practice* is defined as systematic exercise to gain proficiency. In other words, repeated drill brings improvement. You know from your own experience that when you practice anything—from piano to basketball—you become better at it. The same holds true for reading. As you are doing the drills and exercises in these books, you are practicing *all* of your reading skills at the same time. With practice you become a fluent reader and comprehender—a better reader of everything you read.

2. Using context. Good readers are aware of context and use it to aid understanding. Context refers to the words surrounding those you are reading. Meaning, you see, does not come from a single word, or even a single sentence—it is conveyed within the whole context of what you are reading.

The language of literature is rich with meaning. The storyteller is trying to *please* the reader, not *teach* the reader. The writer wants to share feelings and experiences with the reader, to reach him or her in a personal way. As you practice reading literature, you are developing your skill in using context to extract the full measure of meaning and appreciation. These same context skills can be put to work when you are reading textbooks to help you organize facts into a meaningful body of knowledge.

3. Vocabulary growth. Our early vocabulary comes from listening—to our families, friends, television, teachers, and classmates. We learn and understand new words as we hear them being used by others. In fact, the more times we encounter a word, the better we understand it. Finally, it becomes ours, part of our permanent vocabulary of words we know and use.

As time goes by, an increasing number of words is introduced to us through recreational reading. Most of the words we know come from reading—words we have never looked up in a dictionary, but whose meanings have become clear to us through seeing them again and again until they are finally ours. Literature, the kind you will be reading in this book, provides countless opportunities for meeting and learning new words. Literature, as you have seen, also provides the context for seeing these new words used with precision and effect. As you work through the pages in this book, you will be developing a larger and stronger vocabulary—a storehouse of words that become your tools for learning.

4. Skills transfer. You are using this book to develop your ability to read literature with increased speed and comprehension. With regular practice and a little effort, you will be successful in reaching that goal.

As we mentioned, you will also be improving your context skills and building a bigger vocabulary. These are all wonderful results from using this book.

But, perhaps the greatest benefit of all is the application of these improvements to all of your reading tasks, not just literature. Using this book will make you a better reader, and *better readers read everything better.*

Reading Literature Faster

Through literature we share an experience with a writer. That experience may be presented as a conversation, a character or scene, an emotion, or an event.

Let's examine these four kinds of presentation. Let's see if there are characteristics or clues we can use to help us identify each kind. Once we know what we are expected to experience, we can read more intelligently and more quickly.

When you are working in this book, your instructor will schedule a few moments for you to preview each selection before timing begins. Use the preview time to scan the selection rapidly, looking for one of the following kinds of presentation.

1. Reading and Understanding a Conversation

A conversation is intended to tell us what characters are thinking or feeling—the best way to do this is through their own words.

Read the following conversation between George and his mother, an excerpt from "George's Mother" by Stephen Crane:

> Finally he said savagely: "Damn these early hours!" His mother jumped as if he had thrown a missile at her. "Why, George—" she began.
>
> George broke in again. "Oh, I know all that—but this gettin' up in th' mornin' so early just makes me sick. Jest when a man is gettin' his mornin' nap he's gotta get up. I—"
>
> "George, dear," said his mother, "yeh know I hate yeh to swear, dear. Now, please don't." She looked beseechingly at him.
>
> He made a swift gesture. "Well, I ain't swearin', am I?" he demanded. "I was only sayin' that this gettin'-up business gives me a pain, wasn't I?"
>
> "Well, yeh know how swearin' hurts me," protested the little old woman. She seemed about to sob. She gazed off . . . apparently recalling persons who had never been profane.

First, is this a conversation? Yes, we know it is. There are quotation marks throughout indicating words spoken by the characters. So, to identify a conversation, we look for quotation marks.

Next, does this conversation tell us what the characters are thinking or feeling? It certainly does—this conversation is unmistakably clear. We know how George *feels* about getting up in the morning, and we know how his mother *feels* about profanity.

Finally, how should we read this and other conversations we encounter in literature? Join the conversation; pretend you are one of the speakers and that these are your own words. Listen to the other character as though words are being addressed to you.

Conversations can be read quickly and understood well when you recognize them and become part of them.

2. Reading About and Understanding a Character or Scene

How do we learn about a character? There are many ways. Writers introduce characters (1) by telling us what they look like; (2) by what they say; (3) by the things they do; and (4) by telling us what others think and say about them:

> He was a staid, placid gentleman, something past the prime of life, yet upright in his carriage for all that, and slim as a greyhound. He was well mounted upon a sturdy chestnut cob, and had the graceful seat of an experienced horseman; while his riding gear, though free from such fopperies as were then in vogue, was handsome and well chosen. He wore a riding coat of a somewhat brighter green than might have been expected to suit the taste of a gentleman of his years, with a short, black velvet cape, and laced pocket holes and cuffs, all of a jaunty fashion; his linen too, was of the finest kind, worked in a rich pattern at the wrists and throat, and scrupulously white. Although he seemed, judging from the mud he had picked up on the way, to have come from London, his horse was as smooth and cool as his own iron-gray periwig and pigtail.

Obviously a character is being introduced to us in this passage from *Barnaby Rudge* by Charles Dickens. We are told how he carries himself and how he is dressed. We even know a little about what he has been doing.

The question to ask yourself is: Is this character lifelike and real? Real characters should be like real people—good and bad, happy and sad, alike and different. In reading about characters, look for the same details you look for in all people.

Similarly, when a scene or location is being described, look for words which tell about size, shape, color, appearance. Such descriptor words help us picture in our minds the place being described. Try to visualize the scene as you read.

3. Experiencing an Emotion Through Literature

When a writer presents an emotion for us to experience, the intent is to produce an effect within us. The intended effect may be pity, fear, revulsion, or some other emotion. The writer wants us to *feel* something.

In the following passage from *Jane Eyre* by Charlotte Brontë, what emotions are we expected to feel for the character?

> John had not much affection for his mother and sisters, and an antipathy to me. He bullied and punished me; not two or three times in the week, not once or twice in the day, but continually: every nerve I had feared him, and every morsel of flesh on my bones shrank when he came near. There were moments when I was bewildered by the terror he inspired, because I had no appeal whatever against either his menaces or his inflictions; the servants did not like to offend their young master by taking my part against him, and Mrs. Reed was blind and deaf on the subject: She never saw him strike or heard him abuse me, though he did both now and then in her very presence; more frequently behind her back.

Do you feel sorry for this girl because she is being abused? Do you feel compassion because she is suffering? Are you suffering with her? Do you feel anger toward her abuser? What other effects are intended? How are these effects produced?

Emotional and provocative words and expressions have been employed by the writer to paint a vivid portrait of her character's predicament. Can you identify some of the words? What did John do? He *bullied*, *struck*, *punished*, and *abused*. The girl felt fear, bewilderment, and terror. These very expressive and emotional words and phrases are the clues provided by the writer to help her readers read and comprehend effectively.

4. Reading About and Understanding an Event

In describing an event—a series of actions—the writer is telling us a story, and the elements of the story are presented in some kind of order or pattern. Read this passage from *Around the World in Eighty Days* by Jules Verne:

> Mr. Fogg and his two companions took their places on a bench opposite the desks of the magistrate and his clerk. Immediately after, Judge Obadiah, a fat, round man, followed by the clerk, entered. He proceeded to take down a wig which was hanging on a nail, and put it hurriedly on his head.
>
> "The first case," said he. Then, putting his hand to his head, he exclaimed "Heh! This is not my wig!"
>
> "No, your worship," returned the clerk, "it is mine."
>
> "My dear Mr. Oysterpuff, how can a judge give a wise sentence in a clerk's wig?"
>
> The wigs were exchanged.

Did you see how this little story was told? The events in the story were presented in chronological order—from first to last as they occurred. This is a frequently used and easily recognized pattern, but not the only one writers use. The story could have been told in reverse—the story could have opened with the judge wearing the wrong wig and then gone on to explain how the mistake happened.

In passages like these, look for the events in the story and see how they are related, how one event follows or builds on the other. By recognizing the pattern of storytelling and using the pattern as an aid to organizing and understanding the events, you can become a better and faster reader.

How to Use This Book

1 Read the lessons
First, read the lessons on pages 8 through 11. These lessons teach you how to recognize and identify the kinds of presentation you encounter in literature and in the selections in this book.

2 Preview
Find a literature selection to read and wait for your instructor's signal to preview. You will have 30 seconds to preview (scan) the selection to identify the author's kind of presentation.

3 Begin reading
When your instructor gives you the signal, begin reading. Read at a slightly faster-than-normal speed. Read well enough so that you will be able to answer questions about what you have read.

7 Fill in the progress graph
Enter your score and plot your reading time on the graph on page 118 or 119. The right-hand side of the graph shows your words-per-minute reading speed. Write this number at the bottom of the page on the line labeled *Words per Minute.*

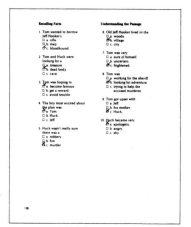

4 Record your time

When you finish reading, look at the blackboard and note your reading time. Your reading time will be the lowest time remaining on the board, or the next number to be erased. Write this time at the bottom of the page on the line labeled *Reading Time*.

5 Answer the questions

Answer the ten questions on the next page. There are five fact questions and five thought questions. Pick the *best* answer to each question and put an x in the box beside it.

6 Correct your answers

Using the Answer Key on pages 116 and 117, correct your work. Circle your wrong answers and put an x in the box you should have marked. Score 10 points for each correct answer. Write your score at the bottom of the page on the line labeled *Comprehension Score*.

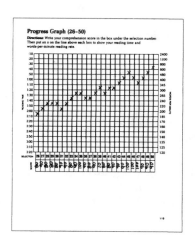

Instructions for the Pacing Drills

From time to time your instructor may wish to conduct pacing drills using *Timed Readings*. For this work you need to use the Pacing Dots printed in the margins of your book pages. The dots will help you regulate your reading speed to match the pace set by your instructor or announced on the reading cassette tape.

Pacing Dots

You will be reading at the correct pace if you are at the dot when your instructor says "Mark" or when you hear a tone on the tape. If you are ahead of the pace, read a little more slowly; if you are behind the pace, increase your reading speed. Try to match the pace exactly.

Follow these steps.

Step 1: Record the pace. At the bottom of the page, write on the line labeled *Words per Minute* the rate announced by the instructor or by the speaker on the tape.

Step 2: Begin reading. Wait for the signal to begin reading. Read at a slightly faster-than-normal speed. You will not know how on-target your pace is until you hear your instructor say "Mark" or until you hear the first tone on the tape. After a little practice you will be able to select an appropriate starting speed most of the time.

Step 3: Adjust your pace. As you read, try to match the pace set by the instructor or the tape. Read more slowly or more quickly as necessary. You should be reading the line beside the dot when you hear the pacing signal. The pacing sounds may distract you at first. Don't worry about it. Keep reading and your concentration will return.

Step 4: Stop and answer questions. Stop reading when you are told to, even if you have not finished the selection. Answer the questions right away. Correct your work and record your score on the line *Comprehension Score*. Strive to maintain 80 percent comprehension on each drill as you gradually increase your pace.

Step 5: Fill in the pacing graph. Transfer your words-per-minute rate to the box labeled *Pace* on the pacing graph on page 120. Then plot your comprehension score on the line above the box.

These pacing drills are designed to help you become a more flexible reader. They encourage you to "break out" of a pattern of reading everything at the same speed.

The drills help in other ways, too. Sometimes in a reading program you reach a certain level and bog down. You don't seem able to move on and progress. The pacing drills will help you to work your way out of such slumps and get your reading program moving again.

For more than a year after the publication of *Diadems and Faggots* the letters, the inane indiscriminate letters of commendation, of criticism, of interrogation, had poured in on Geoffrey Betton by every post. Hundreds of unknown readers had told him with unsparing detail all that his book had been to them. And the wonder of it was, when all was said and done, that it had really been so little—that when their thick broth of praise was strained through the author's searching vanity there remained to him so small a sediment of definite specific understanding! No—it was always the same thing, over and over and over again—the same vague gush of adjectives, the same incorrigible tendency to estimate his effort according to each writer's personal preferences, instead of regarding it as a work of art, a thing to be measured by fixed standards!

He smiled to think how little, at first, he had felt the vanity of it all. He had found a saviour even in the grosser evidences of popularity: the advertisements of his book, the daily shower of "clippings," the sense that, when he entered a restaurant or a theater, people nudged each other and said "That's Geoffrey Betton." Yes, the publicity had been sweet to him—at first. He had been touched by the sympathy of his fellow men: had thought indulgently of the world, as a better place than the failures and the dyspeptics would acknowledge. And then his success began to submerge him: he gasped under the thickening shower of letters. His admirers were really unappeasable. And they wanted him to do such ridiculous things—to give lectures, to head movements, to be tendered receptions, to speak at banquets, to address mothers, to plead for orphans, to go up in balloons, to lead the struggle for sterilized milk. They wanted his photograph for literary supplements, his autograph for charity bazaars, his name on committees, literary, educational, and social; above all, they wanted his opinion on everything: on Christianity, on Buddhism, on tight lacing, on the drug habit, on democratic government, on female suffrage, and on love. Perhaps the chief benefit of this demand was his incidentally learning from it how few opinions he really had: the only one that remained with him was a rooted horror of all forms of correspondence. He had been unspeakably thankful when the letters began to fall off.

Recalling Facts

1. *Diadems and Faggots* was a
   - ☐ a. play.
   - ☐ b. poem.
   - ☐ c. book.

2. Geoffrey Betton felt that his fans lacked
   - ☐ a. formal education.
   - ☐ b. a sense of fairness.
   - ☐ c. real understanding.

3. Geoffrey thought his work should be judged by
   - ☐ a. personal preference.
   - ☐ b. fixed standards.
   - ☐ c. popular appeal.

4. At first Geoffrey
   - ☐ a. loved the publicity.
   - ☐ b. hated the publicity.
   - ☐ c. ignored the publicity.

5. Above all, people wanted Geoffrey's
   - ☐ a. autograph.
   - ☐ b. photograph.
   - ☐ c. opinions.

Understanding the Passage

6. It seems that *Diadems and Faggots* had been a
   - ☐ a. publishing failure.
   - ☐ b. modest success.
   - ☐ c. major hit.

7. Geoffrey thought his readers took his writing too
   - ☐ a. seriously.
   - ☐ b. personally.
   - ☐ c. lightly.

8. Geoffrey did not handle very well his
   - ☐ a. success.
   - ☐ b. money.
   - ☐ c. both a and b.

9. Apparently Geoffrey was a
   - ☐ a. publicity seeker.
   - ☐ b. gifted speaker.
   - ☐ c. private person.

10. Geoffrey's range of interests was
   - ☐ a. broader than his readers expected.
   - ☐ b. all that his readers expected.
   - ☐ c. narrower than his readers suspected.

from **Belphagor** *by Niccolò Machiavelli*

We read in the ancient archives of Florence the following account, as it was received from the lips of a very holy man, greatly respected by everyone for the sanctity of his manners at the period in which he lived. Happening once to be deeply absorbed in his prayers, such was their efficacy, that he saw an infinite number of condemned souls, belonging to those miserable mortals who had died in their sins, undergoing the punishments due to their offences in the regions below. He remarked that the greater part of them lamented nothing so bitterly as their folly in having taken wives, attributing to them the whole of their misfortunes. Much surprised at this, Minos and Rhadamanthus, with the rest of the infernal judges, unwilling to credit all the abuse heaped upon the female sex, and wearied from day to day with its repetition, agreed to bring the matter before Pluto. It was then resolved that the conclave of infernal princes should form a committee of inquiry, and should adopt such measures as might be deemed most advisable by the court in order to discover the truth or falsehood of the calumnies which they heard. All being assembled in council, Pluto addressed them as follows: "Deadly beloved demons! Though by celestial dispensation and the irreversible decree of fate this kingdom fell to my share, and I might strictly dispense with any kind of celestial or earthly responsibility, yet, as it is more prudent and respectful to consult the laws and to hear the opinion of others, I have resolved to be guided by your advice, particularly in a case that may chance to cast some imputation upon our government. For the souls of all men daily arriving in our kingdom still continue to lay the whole blame upon their wives, and as this appears to us impossible, we must be careful how we decide in such a business, lest we also should come in for a share of their abuse, on account of our too great severity; and yet judgment must be pronounced, lest we be taxed with negligence and with indifference to the interests of justice. Now, as the latter is the fault of a careless, and the former of an unjust judge, we, wishing to avoid the trouble and the blame that might attach to both naturally enough apply to you for assistance."

Recalling Facts

1. The very holy man saw an infinite number of
   - ☐ a. archives.
   - ☐ b. condemned souls.
   - ☐ c. offences against the gods.

2. Most of the condemned men blamed their
   - ☐ a. bad fortune.
   - ☐ b. wives.
   - ☐ c. government.

3. Minos and Rhadamanthus were
   - ☐ a. judges.
   - ☐ b. evil men.
   - ☐ c. divorce attorneys.

4. The infernal princes agreed to form a committee of
   - ☐ a. justice.
   - ☐ b. correspondence.
   - ☐ c. inquiry.

5. The chief ruler of the kingdom was
   - ☐ a. Pluto.
   - ☐ b. Minos.
   - ☐ c. Rhadamanthus.

Understanding the Passage

6. The "regions below" refers to
   - ☐ a. a penal colony.
   - ☐ b. the county courtroom.
   - ☐ c. hell.

7. The dead men were
   - ☐ a. unashamed.
   - ☐ b. regretful.
   - ☐ c. kind.

8. Minos and Rhadamanthus were trying to
   - ☐ a. ignore the complaints of the dead men.
   - ☐ b. be fair to females.
   - ☐ c. avoid the wrath of Pluto.

9. Pluto got his position through
   - ☐ a. the will of fate.
   - ☐ b. regular elections among demons.
   - ☐ c. steady promotions.

10. Pluto wanted to
    - ☐ a. share the blame.
    - ☐ b. hear the opinions of his fellow demons.
    - ☐ c. both a and b.

One of the phenomena which had peculiarly attracted my attention was the structure of the human frame and, indeed, any animal endued with life. Whence, I often asked myself, did the principle of life proceed? It was a bold question, and one which has ever been considered as a mystery; yet with how many things are we upon the brink of becoming acquainted, if cowardice or carelessness did not restrain our inquiries. I revolved these circumstances in my mind, and determined to apply myself more particularly to those branches of natural philosophy which relate to physiology. Unless I had been animated by an almost supernatural enthusiasm, my application to this study would have been irksome, and almost intolerable. To examine the causes of life, we must first have recourse to death. I became acquainted with the science of anatomy: but this was not sufficient; I must also observe the natural decay and corruption of the human body. In my education my father had taken care that my mind should be impressed with no supernatural horrors. I do not ever remember to have trembled at a tale of superstition, or to have feared the apparition of a spirit. Darkness had no effect upon my fancy; and a churchyard was to me merely the receptacle of bodies deprived of life, which, from being the seat of beauty and strength, had become food for the worm. Now I was led to examine the cause and progress of this decay, and forced to spend days and nights in vaults and charnel houses. My attention was fixed upon every object the most insupportable to the delicacy of the human feelings. I saw how the fine form of man was degraded and wasted; I beheld the corruption of death succeed the blooming cheek of life; I saw how the worm inherited the wonders of the eye and brain. I paused, examining and analyzing all the minutiae of causation, as exemplified in the change from life to death, and death to life, until from the midst of this darkness a sudden light broke in upon me—a light so brilliant and wondrous, yet so simple, that while I became dizzy with the immensity of the prospect which it illustrated, I was surprised, that among so many men of genius who had directed their inquiries towards the same science, that I alone should be reserved to discover so astonishing a secret.

Recalling Facts

1. The narrator often asked himself questions about
   - ☐ a. the principles of life.
   - ☐ b. the structure of government.
   - ☐ c. both a and b.

2. The narrator was very
   - ☐ a. confused.
   - ☐ b. weak willed.
   - ☐ c. determined.

3. The narrator was particularly interested in
   - ☐ a. psychology.
   - ☐ b. sociology.
   - ☐ c. physiology.

4. The narrator's father taught him not to be
   - ☐ a. superstitious.
   - ☐ b. curious.
   - ☐ c. a bookworm.

5. The narrator spent many nights studying in
   - ☐ a. a biologist's laboratory.
   - ☐ b. the church rectory.
   - ☐ c. vaults and charnel houses.

Understanding the Passage

6. The narrator claimed that research was often
   - ☐ a. interrupted by lack of money.
   - ☐ b. hurt by lack of nerve.
   - ☐ c. productive if you knew what you were doing.

7. The narrator can best be described as
   - ☐ a. single-minded.
   - ☐ b. unambitious.
   - ☐ c. religious.

8. The most important part of the narrator's study was
   - ☐ a. anatomy.
   - ☐ b. gravedigging.
   - ☐ c. the decay of a dead body

9. The narrator viewed graveyards with great
   - ☐ a. fear.
   - ☐ b. revulsion.
   - ☐ c. objectivity.

10. At the end of the passage, the narrator
    - ☐ a. became physically ill.
    - ☐ b. was blinded by a sudden burst of light.
    - ☐ c. made a great discovery.

At last a cold gray light was visible through the puckers and chinks in the curtains. We yawned and stretched with satisfaction, shed our cocoons, and felt that we had slept as much as was necessary. As the sun rose up and warmed the world, we pulled off our blankets and got ready for breakfast. We were just pleasantly in time, for five minutes afterward the driver sent the weird music of his bugle winding over the grassy solitudes, and presently we detected a low hut or two in the distance. Then the rattling of the coach, the clatter of our six horses' hooves, and the driver's crisp commands, awoke to a louder and stronger emphasis, and we went sweeping down on the station at our smartest speed. It was fascinating—that old Overland stage coaching.

The driver tossed his gathered reins out on the ground, gaped and stretched complacently, drew off his heavy buckskin gloves with great deliberation and insufferable dignity—taking not the slightest notice of a dozen solicitous inquiries after his health, and humbly facetious and flattering accostings, and obsequious tenders of service, from five or six hairy and half-civilized station keepers and hostlers who were nimbly unhitching our steeds and bringing the fresh team out of the stables—for, in the eyes of the stage driver, station keepers and hostlers were a sort of good enough low creature, useful in their place, and helping to make up a world, but not the kind of beings which a person of distinction could afford to concern himself with; while, on the contrary, in the eyes of the station keeper and the hostler, the stage driver was a hero—a great and shining dignitary, the world's favorite son, the envy of the people, the ob- served of the nations. When they spoke to him they received his insolent silence meekly, and as being the natural and proper conduct of so great a man; when he opened his lips they all hung on his words with admiration (he never honored a particular individual with a remark, but addressed it with a broad generality to the horses, the stables, the surrounding country *and* the human underlings); when he discharged a facetious insulting personality at a hostler, that hostler was happy for the day; when he uttered his one jest, coarse, profane, witless, and inflicted on the same audience every time his coach drove up there—the varlets roared.

Recalling Facts

1. The narrator had gotten
   - □ a. too much sleep.
   - □ b. enough sleep.
   - □ c. too little sleep.

2. The driver signaled his arrival with a
   - □ a. drum.
   - □ b. bugle.
   - □ c. whistle.

3. The stagecoach was pulled by
   - □ a. four horses.
   - □ b. six horses.
   - □ c. eight horses.

4. The station keeper and the hostler viewed the stage driver as
   - □ a. a nuisance.
   - □ b. an honest co-worker.
   - □ c. a great dignitary.

5. The stage driver's one joke was
   - □ a. witless.
   - □ b. subtle.
   - □ c. original.

Understanding the Passage

6. The narrator had slept
   - □ a. in a hostel.
   - □ b. next to the stage driver.
   - □ c. inside the stagecoach.

7. The narrator found stage coaching
   - □ a. captivating.
   - □ b. mildly interesting.
   - □ c. routine and boring.

8. The driver
   - □ a. mostly ignored the townspeople.
   - □ b. knew the townspeople well.
   - □ c. chatted insincerely with the townspeople.

9. To the stage driver, station keepers and hostlers were
   - □ a. very important people.
   - □ b. worthless varlets.
   - □ c. useful but socially intolerable.

10. The townspeople
   - □ a. appreciated whatever the stage driver did.
   - □ b. protested against the stage driver's insolence.
   - □ c. rarely laughed at the stage driver's jokes.

from **Don Quixote** *by Miguel de Cervantes*

For four days was Don Quixote most sumptuously entertained in Don Diego's house, at the end of which time he asked his permission to depart, telling him he thanked him for the kindness and hospitality he had received in his house, but that, as it did not become knights-errant to give themselves up for long to idleness and luxury, he was anxious to fulfill the duties of his calling in seeking adventures, of which he was informed there was an abundance in that neighborhood, where he hoped to employ his time until the day came round for the jousts at Saragossa, for that was his proper destination; and that, first of all, he meant to enter the cave of Montesinos, of which so many marvelous things were reported all through the country, and at the same time to investigate and explore the origin and true source of the seven lakes commonly called the lakes of Ruidera.

Don Diego and his son commended his laudable resolution, and bade him furnish himself with all he wanted from their house and belongings, as they would most gladly be of service to him; which, indeed, his personal worth and his honorable profession made it incumbent upon them to be.

The day of his departure came at length, as welcome to Don Quixote as it was sorrowful to his servant, Sancho Panza, who was very well satisfied with the abundance of Don Diego's house, and objected to return to the starvation of the woods and wilds and the shortcomings of his ill-stocked packs; these, however, he filled and packed with what he considered most needful. On taking leave, Don Quixote said earnestly, "If you wish to spare yourself fatigue and toil in reaching the inaccessible summit of the temple of fame, you have nothing to do but turn aside out of the somewhat narrow path of poetry and take the still narrower one of knight-errantry, wide enough, however, to make you an emperor in the twinkling of an eye."

In this speech Don Quixote increased the evidence of his madness. Both Don Diego and his son were amazed afresh at the strange medley Don Quixote talked, at one moment sense, at another nonsense, and at the pertinacity and persistence he displayed in going through thick and thin in quest of his unlucky adventures, which he made the end and aim of his desires.

Recalling Facts

1. Don Quixote stayed with
   Don Diego for
   ☐ a. four days.
   ☐ b. six days.
   ☐ c. ten days.

2. Don Quixote thanked
   Don Diego for his
   ☐ a. information.
   ☐ b. hospitality.
   ☐ c. honesty.

3. Don Quixote was looking
   forward to the
   ☐ a. day of his retirement.
   ☐ b. jousts at Saragossa.
   ☐ c. return to Don Diego's.

4. The idea of leaving
   Don Diego's house filled
   Sancho with
   ☐ a. panic.
   ☐ b. sadness.
   ☐ c. relief.

5. Don Quixote felt it was
   his duty to
   ☐ a. seek out adventures.
   ☐ b. be strict with Sancho Panza.
   ☐ c. expose the duplicity of
      Don Diego.

Understanding the Passage

6. Don Quixote apparently
   did not
   ☐ a. have any servants.
   ☐ b. like Don Diego.
   ☐ c. stay in one place
      very long.

7. Sancho Panza was attracted
   by the idea of
   ☐ a. adventure.
   ☐ b. security.
   ☐ c. solitude.

8. Don Diego appeared to be a
   ☐ a. traveling speaker.
   ☐ b. knight-errant.
   ☐ c. poet.

9. Don Diego and his son
   thought Don Quixote was
   ☐ a. interesting.
   ☐ b. moronic.
   ☐ c. rude.

10. Don Quixote believed that
    the life of a knight-errant was
    ☐ a. profitable.
    ☐ b. noble.
    ☐ c. frivolous.

from **Ormond** *by Maria Edgeworth*

During the course of Ormond's tour through Ireland, he frequently found himself in company with those who knew the history of public affairs for years past, and were but too well acquainted with the political profligacy and shameful jobbing of Sir Ulick O'Shane.

Some of these gentlemen, knowing Mr. Ormond to be his ward, refrained, or course, from touching upon any subject relative to Sir Ulick; and when Ormond mentioned him, evaded the conversation, or agreed in general terms in praising his abilities, wit, and address. But, after a day or two's journey, when he was beyond his own and the adjoining counties, when he went into company with those who happened to know nothing of his connection with Sir Ulick O'Shane, then he heard him spoken of in a very different manner. He was quite astonished and dismayed by the general abuse which was poured upon him.

"Well, every man of abilities excites envy—every man who takes a part in politics, especially in times when parties run high, must expect to be abused: they must bear it, and their friends must learn to bear it for them."

Such were the reflections with which Ormond at first comforted himself. As far as party abuse went, this was quite satisfactory; even facts, or what are told as facts, are so altered by the manner of seeing them by an opposite party, that, without meaning to traduce, they calumniate. Ormond entrenched himself in disbelief, and cool assertion of his disbelief, of a variety of anecdotes he continually heard discreditable to Sir Ulick. Still he expected that, when he went into other company, and met with men of Sir Ulick's own party, he should obtain proofs of the falsehood of these stories, and by that he might be able not only to contradict, but to confute them. People, however, only smiled and told him that he had better inquire no farther, if he expected to find Sir Ulick an immaculate character. Those who liked him best laughed off the notorious instances of his public defection of principle, and of his private jobbing, as good jokes; proofs of his knowledge of the world—his address, his frankness, his being "not a bit of a hypocrite." But even those who professed to like him best, and to be the least scrupulous with regard to public virtue, still spoke with facetious contempt of Sir Ulick.

Recalling Facts

1. Ormond was Ulick O'Shane's
   - ☐ a. campaign manager.
   - ☐ b. nephew.
   - ☐ c. ward.

2. People who knew of Ormond's relationship to Sir Ulick were
   - ☐ a. especially harsh in criticizing Ulick.
   - ☐ b. tactful when speaking of him around Ormond.
   - ☐ c. stunned to learn that Ormond was in Ireland.

3. Ormond hoped to get proof that Sir Ulick was
   - ☐ a. an honorable politician.
   - ☐ b. a corrupt politician.
   - ☐ c. a popular politician.

4. Sir Ulick's best supporters praised him for his
   - ☐ a. frankness.
   - ☐ b. honesty.
   - ☐ c. scruples.

5. Ormond expected people from the opposing party to
   - ☐ a. criticize Sir Ulick.
   - ☐ b. vote for Sir Ulick.
   - ☐ c. respect Sir Ulick.

Understanding the Passage

6. Before his travels, Ormond knew
   - ☐ a. Sir Ulick was not going to be reelected.
   - ☐ b. nothing of Sir Ulick's shady deeds.
   - ☐ c. Sir Ulick was going to meet him in Dublin.

7. Apparently no one in Ireland believed
   - ☐ a. Sir Ulick was honest.
   - ☐ b. Ormond was related to Sir Ulick.
   - ☐ c. Ormond had come from America.

8. When Ormond first heard attacks against Sir Ulick, he
   - ☐ a. refused to believe them.
   - ☐ b. did some quick research into Irish politics.
   - ☐ c. demanded explanations.

9. Ormond was most shocked by the attitude of
   - ☐ a. members of the opposing party.
   - ☐ b. Sir Ulick's own party members.
   - ☐ c. Sir Ulick himself.

10. Ormond's travels
    - ☐ a. led him to join the opposition party.
    - ☐ b. gave him distressing information about Sir Ulick.
    - ☐ c. convinced him to work on Sir Ulick's behalf.

The student may read Homer or Aeschylus in the Greek without danger of dissipation of luxuriousness, for it implies that he in some measure emulates their heroes, and consecrates morning hours to their pages. The heroic books, even if printed in the character of our mother tongue, will always be in a language dead to degenerate times; and we must laboriously seek the meaning of each word, conjecturing a larger sense than common use permits out of what wisdom and valor and generosity we have. The modern cheap and fertile press, with all its translations, has done little to bring us nearer to the heroic writers of antiquity. They seem as solitary, and the letter in which they are printed as rare and curious, as ever. It is worth the expense of youthful days and costly hours, if you learn only some words of an ancient language, which are raised out of the trivialness of the street, to be perpetual suggestions and provocations. It is not in vain that the farmer remembers and repeats the few Latin words which he has heard. Men sometimes speak as if the study of the classics would at length make way for more modern and practical studies; but the adventurous student will always study classics, in whatever language they may be written and however ancient they may be. For what are the classics but the noblest recorded thoughts of man? They are the only oracles which are not decayed, and there are such answers to the most modern inquiry in them as Delphi and Dodona never gave. To read well, that is, to read true books in a true spirit, is a noble exercise, and one that will task the reader more than any other exercise which the customs of the day esteem. It requires a training such as the athletes underwent, the steady intention almost of the whole life to this object. Books must be read as deliberately and reservedly as they were written. It isn't enough to speak the language of that nation by which they are written, for there is a memorable interval between the spoken and the written language, the language heard and the language read. The one is commonly transitory, a dialect merely, almost brutish, which we learn unconsciously of our mothers; the other is the maturity and experience of that, a reserved and select expression, too significant to be heard by the ear.

Recalling Facts

1. The narrator regards the writers of antiquity as
   - ☐ a. immortal.
   - ☐ b. heroic.
   - ☐ c. both a and b.

2. According to the narrator, the modern press has
   - ☐ a. promoted ancient works.
   - ☐ b. done little to promote the classics.
   - ☐ c. flatly refused to print the classics.

3. The narrator believes that learning a few words of Latin is
   - ☐ a. a waste of time.
   - ☐ b. all that is needed to be successful in life.
   - ☐ c. helpful.

4. The narrator states that reading the classics
   - ☐ a. requires great effort.
   - ☐ b. prepares one for practical studies.
   - ☐ c. both a and b.

5. The narrator feels there is a great difference between
   - ☐ a. Greek and Latin writers.
   - ☐ b. the spoken language and the written language.
   - ☐ c. athletes and students of the classics.

Understanding the Passage

6. According to the narrator, it is a noble exercise to
   - ☐ a. have a large family.
   - ☐ b. study the truth.
   - ☐ c. acquire fame.

7. The narrator feels that
   - ☐ a. more and more people are reading the classics.
   - ☐ b. no one is reading the classics anymore.
   - ☐ c. only a few people are reading the classics.

8. The narrator believes people should read the classics
   - ☐ a. to get better jobs.
   - ☐ b. to become better farmers.
   - ☐ c. for personal betterment.

9. Reading the classics is described as
   - ☐ a. very difficult, but worthwhile.
   - ☐ b. impossible for most people.
   - ☐ c. a good leisure time activity.

10. The narrator believes that the written language is
   - ☐ a. inferior to the spoken language.
   - ☐ b. indistinguishable from the spoken language.
   - ☐ c. superior to the spoken language.

8 *from* **A Journal of the Plague Year** *by Daniel Defoe*

The Lord Mayor and the sheriffs, the Court of Aldermen, and a certain number of the Common Council men, or their deputies, came to a resolution and published it. They would not quit the city themselves, but they would be always at hand for preserving good order in every place and for doing justice on all occasions; and also for distributing the public charity to the poor; and, in a word, for doing the duty and discharging the trust reposed in them by the citizens, despite the ravages of the plague.

In pursuance of these orders, the Lord Mayor, sheriffs, and councilmen held councils every day, more or less, for making such dispositions as they found needful for preserving the civil peace; and though they used the people with all possible gentleness and clemency, yet all manner of presumptuous rogues, such as thieves, housebreakers, plunderers of the dead or of the sick, were duly punished, and several declarations were continually published by the Lord Mayor and Court of Aldermen against such.

Also all constables and churchwardens were enjoined to stay in the city upon severe penalties, or to depute such able and sufficient housekeepers as the deputy aldermen or Common Council men of the precinct should approve, and for whom they should give security; and also security in case of mortality, that they would forthwith constitute other constables in their stead.

These things reestablished the minds of the people very much, especially in the first of their fright, when they talked of making so universal a flight that the city would have been in danger of being entirely deserted of its inhabitants, except the poor, and the country of being plundered and laid waste by the multitude. Nor were the magistrates deficient in performing their part as boldly as they promised it; for my Lord Mayor and the sheriffs were continually in the streets, and at places of the greatest danger, and though they did not care for having too great a resort of people crowding about them, yet in emergent cases they never denied the people access to them, and heard with patience all their grievances and complaints. My Lord Mayor had a low gallery built on purpose in his hall, where he stood away from the crowd when any complaint came to be heard, that he might appear with as much safety as possible.

Recalling Facts

1. The leading city officials promised to
   - ☐ a. stay in town.
   - ☐ b. run for reelection.
   - ☐ c. serve without pay.

2. The Lord Mayor and other city officials held councils nearly every
   - ☐ a. day.
   - ☐ b. week.
   - ☐ c. month.

3. The city officials worked especially hard to
   - ☐ a. improve sanitation.
   - ☐ b. control animals.
   - ☐ c. preserve civil peace.

4. The actions of city officials
   - ☐ a. frightened the people.
   - ☐ b. reassured the people.
   - ☐ c. perplexed the people.

5. To separate himself from the crowd, the Lord Mayor built a
   - ☐ a. wall.
   - ☐ b. curtain.
   - ☐ c. gallery.

Understanding the Passage

6. This passage suggests that the city officials were
   - ☐ a. excellent leaders.
   - ☐ b. mediocre leaders.
   - ☐ c. ineffective leaders.

7. The city officials dealt with housebreakers
   - ☐ a. with great clemency.
   - ☐ b. by ignoring them.
   - ☐ c. harshly.

8. Lower officials who left the city were
   - ☐ a. immediately fired.
   - ☐ b. refused promotions.
   - ☐ c. punished severely.

9. At first, city officials feared that
   - ☐ a. nearly everyone would flee the town.
   - ☐ b. country folks would overrun the city.
   - ☐ c. a great fire would probably break out.

10. The city officials did not want to get too close to the people because they feared
   - ☐ a. pickpockets.
   - ☐ b. getting the plague.
   - ☐ c. assassination.

The chaplain approached the harpsichord and pretended to listen atten-
tively to Amelia's performance. The rest of the family made a half circle
at a little distance, waiting respectfully for the judgment which Consuelo
would pronounce upon her pupil.

Amelia bravely chose an air from the *Achille in Scyro* of Pergolese, and
sang it with assurance from beginning to end in a shrill and piercing voice,
accompanied by a German accent so comic, that Consuelo, who had never
heard anything of the kind, was hardly able to keep from smiling at every
word. It was barely necessary to hear four bars, to be convinced that the
young baroness had no true notion, no knowledge of music. She had a
flexible voice, and perhaps had received good lessons; but her character
was too frivolous to allow her to study anything conscientiously. For the
same reason, she did not mistrust her own powers, and attempted the
boldest and most difficult passages. She failed in all, and thought to cover
her unskillfulness by forcing her pronunciation, and banging the accom-
paniment; restoring the measure as she could, by adding time to the bars
following those in which she had diminished it, and changing the character
of the music to such an extent, that Consuelo could hardly recognize what
she heard, though the pages were before her eyes.

Count Christian, who was quite a connoisseur, but who attributed to his
niece all the timidity he would have felt in her place, said from time to time
to encourage her: "Well, Amelia, very well! Beautiful music!" The canoness,
who did not know much about it, looked with solicitude into the eyes of
Consuelo, in order to foresee her opinion; and the baron, who loved no
other music than the flourishes of the hunting horn, believing that his
daughter sang too well for him to understand, waited in confidence for the
expression of the judge's satisfaction.

Consuelo very clearly saw, that to tell the plain truth would distress the
whole family. Resolving to enlighten her pupil in private upon all those
matters which she had to forget before she could learn anything, she
praised her voice, asked about her studies, approved the choice of masters,
whose works she had been made to study; and thus relieved herself from
the necessity of declaring that she had studied them incorrectly. And so
the family separated, well pleased with what had transpired.

Recalling Facts

1. Amelia sang and played the
   - ☐ a. piano.
   - ☐ b. harpsichord.
   - ☐ c. accordian.

2. Amelia sang with
   - ☐ a. an English accent.
   - ☐ b. a French accent.
   - ☐ c. a German accent.

3. As she performed, Amelia received encouragement from
   - ☐ a. Consuelo.
   - ☐ b. Count Christian.
   - ☐ c. the chaplain.

4. The canoness did not know
   - ☐ a. much about music.
   - ☐ b. Consuelo's musical background.
   - ☐ c. where Amelia had learned to sing.

5. Consuelo praised Amelia's
   - ☐ a. interpretation of the music.
   - ☐ b. singing voice.
   - ☐ c. dedication to her music.

Understanding the Passage

6. When it came to music, the baron
   - ☐ a. knew very little.
   - ☐ b. considered himself a connoisseur.
   - ☐ c. trusted Count Christian's opinion.

7. Consuelo was
   - ☐ a. an accomplished music teacher.
   - ☐ b. the daughter of the canoness.
   - ☐ c. overwhelmed by Amelia's talent.

8. In appraising Amelia's performance, Consuelo tried to be
   - ☐ a. frank.
   - ☐ b. kind.
   - ☐ c. fair.

9. Amelia had
   - ☐ a. confidence in her abilities
   - ☐ b. studied music abroad.
   - ☐ c. asked the chaplain to listen.

10. Consuelo quickly realized that
    - ☐ a. no one would listen to her opinion.
    - ☐ b. Amelia had no real musical sense.
    - ☐ c. the baron was not impressed by the performance.

We wake up with painful auguring, and, after exploring a little to know the cause, find it is the odious news in each day's paper, the infamy that has fallen on Massachusetts, that clouds the daylight and takes away the comfort out of every hour. We shall never feel well again until that detestable Fugitive Slave Law is nullified in Massachusetts and until the Government is assured that once and for all it cannot and shall not be executed here. All I have and all I can do shall be given and done in opposition to the execution of the law. The word *liberty* in the mouth of Mr. Webster sounds like the word *love* in the mouth of a courtesan. Mr. Choate, whose talent consists in a fine choice of words which he can hang indiscriminately on any offender, has pushed the privilege of his profession so far as to ask, "What would the Puritans of 1620 say to the trashy sentimentalism of modern reformers?" And thus the stern old fathers of Massachusetts who, Mr. Choate knows, would have died at the stake before soiling themselves with this damnation, are made to repudiate the "trashy sentimentalism" of the Ten Commandments. The joke is too imprudent. Mr. Webster has deliberately taken out his name from all the files of honor in which he had enrolled it—from all association with liberal, virtuous, and philanthropic men, and read his recantation on his knees at Richmond and Charleston.

The Union! Oh, yes, I prized that, other things being equal; but what is the Union to a man self-condemned, with all sense of self-respect and chance of fair fame cut off—with the names of conscience and religion become bitter ironies, and liberty the ghastly nothing which Mr. Webster means by that word? The worst mischiefs that could follow from Secession and new combination of the smallest fragments of the wreck were slight and medicable to the calamity your Union has brought us. Another year, and a standing army, officered by Southern gentlemen to protect the Commissioners and to hunt the fugitives, will be illustrating the new sweets of Union in Boston, Worcester, and Springfield. Could Mr. Webster obtain now a vote in the State of Massachusetts for the poorest municipal office? Well, is not this a loss inevitable to a bad law?—a law which no man can countenance or abet the execution of?

Recalling Facts

1. The narrator wanted the Fugitive Slave law
   - ☐ a. approved.
   - ☐ b. enforced.
   - ☐ c. nullified.

2. Mr. Webster spoke often about
   - ☐ a. love.
   - ☐ b. sentiment.
   - ☐ c. liberty.

3. The narrator focused on the Fugitive Slave Law in
   - ☐ a. Richmond.
   - ☐ b. Massachusetts.
   - ☐ c. Charleston.

4. The narrator condemned
   - ☐ a. Mr. Webster.
   - ☐ b. slavery.
   - ☐ c. both a and b.

5. The narrator prized
   - ☐ a. slavery.
   - ☐ b. the Union.
   - ☐ c. Mr. Choate's choice of words.

Understanding the Passage

6. The narrator apparently lived
   - ☐ a. in the South.
   - ☐ b. during the days of the Puritans.
   - ☐ c. in Massachusetts.

7. A courtesan is someone who does not value
   - ☐ a. love.
   - ☐ b. liberty.
   - ☐ c. money.

8. Mr. Choate applied the term "trashy sentimentalism" to
   - ☐ a. those who opposed the new law.
   - ☐ b. all slave owners.
   - ☐ c. the commissioners.

9. To the narrator, the Union was worthwhile
   - ☐ a. under any conditions.
   - ☐ b. only if true liberty was preserved.
   - ☐ c. if the rights of slave owners were protected.

10. The narrator suggested that Mr. Webster could not get elected
    - ☐ a. to any office in Massachusetts.
    - ☐ b. President.
    - ☐ c. Mayor of Richmond.

from **The Absentee** *by Maria Edgeworth*

Lady Clonbrony was taken ill the day after her gala; she had caught cold by standing, when much overheated, in a violent draught of wind, paying her parting compliments to the Duke of V____, who thought her a bore, and wished her in heaven all the time for keeping his horses standing. Her ladyship's illness was severe and long; she was confined to her room for some weeks by a rheumatic fever, and an inflammation in her eyes. Every day, when Lord Colambre went to see his mother, he found Miss Nugent in her apartment, and every hour he found fresh reason to admire this charming girl. The affectionate tenderness, the indefatigable patience, the strong attachment she showed for her aunt, actually raised Lady Clonbrony in her son's opinion: he was persuaded she must surely have some good qualities, or she could not have excited such strong affection. A few foibles out of the question, such as her affectation of being English, and other affectations too tedious to mention, Lady Clonbrony was really a good woman, had good principles, moral and religious, and, selfishness not immediately interfering, she was good-natured; and, though her whole soul and attention were so completely absorbed in the duties of acquaintanceship that she did not know it, she really had affections—they were concentrated upon a few near relations. She was extremely fond and extremely proud of her son, and next to her son, she was fonder of her niece than of any other creature. She had received Grace Nugent into her family when she was left an orphan, and deserted by other relations. She had bred her up, and had treated her with constant kindness. This kindness and these obligations had raised the warmest gratitude in Miss Nugent's heart; and it was the strong principle of gratitude which rendered her capable of endurance and exertions seemingly far above her strength. This young lady was not of a robust appearance, though she now underwent extraordinary fatigue. Her aunt could scarcely bear that she should leave her for a moment, so Grace sat up with her many hours every night. Night after night she bore this fatigue; and yet, with little sleep, she preserved her health, at least supported her spirits; and every morning, when Lord Colambre came into his mother's room, he saw Miss Nugent looking as blooming as if she had enjoyed the most refreshing sleep.

Recalling Facts

1. Lady Clonbrony became sick the day
   - ☐ a. before her gala.
   - ☐ b. of her gala.
   - ☐ c. after her gala.

2. The duke in the passage thought Lady Clonbrony was
   - ☐ a. an angel.
   - ☐ b. a bore.
   - ☐ c. a hypocrite.

3. Lady Clonbrony's illness consisted of rheumatic fever and
   - ☐ a. congestive heart failure.
   - ☐ b. overall fatigue.
   - ☐ c. inflammation of the eyes.

4. As a child, Grace Nugent had been
   - ☐ a. rejected by Lady Clonbrony.
   - ☐ b. betrothed to Lord Colambre.
   - ☐ c. orphaned.

5. Grace Nugent spent many hours each night
   - ☐ a. with Lord Colambre.
   - ☐ b. reading before retiring.
   - ☐ c. sitting up.

Understanding the Passage

6. Lord Colambre was impressed by
   - ☐ a. his mother's selflessness.
   - ☐ b. Miss Nugent's dedication.
   - ☐ c. the doctor's care.

7. By nature, Miss Nugent was rather
   - ☐ a. selfish.
   - ☐ b. frail.
   - ☐ c. shy.

8. Before his mother's illness, Lord Colambre apparently
   - ☐ a. spent a great deal of time with Miss Nugent.
   - ☐ b. did not appreciate his mother's good points.
   - ☐ c. had been very sick himself.

9. Miss Nugent's attitude toward her aunt was one of
   - ☐ a. resentment.
   - ☐ b. condescension.
   - ☐ c. devotion.

10. Lady Clonbrony was characterized as
    - ☐ a. principled but often superficial.
    - ☐ b. hopelessly out of touch with the times.
    - ☐ c. flirtatious and impulsive.

The public room of the Black Bear at Cumnor boasted, on the evening which we speak of, no ordinary assemblage of guests. There had been a fair in the neighborhood, and the fabric merchant of Abingdon, with some of the other personages whom the reader has already been made acquainted with, as friends and customers of Giles Gosling, had already formed their wonted circle around the evening fire, and were talking over the news of the day.

A lively, bustling, arch fellow, whose pack and oaken *ellwand*, studded duly with brass points, denoted him to be of Autolycus's profession, occupied a good deal of the attention, and furnished much of the amusement, of the evening. The peddlers of those days, it must be remembered, were men of far greater importance than the degenerate and degraded hawkers of our modern times. It was by means of these peripatetic vendors that the country trade, in the finer manufactures used in female dress particularly, was almost entirely carried on; and if a merchant of this description arrived at the dignity of traveling with a packhorse, he was a person of no small consequence, and company for the most substantial yeoman or Franklin whom he might meet in his wanderings.

The peddler bore, accordingly, an active and unrebuked share in the merriment to which the rafters of the bonny Black Bear of Cumnor resounded. He had his smile with pretty Mistress Cicely, his broad laugh with mine host, and his jest upon dashing Master Goldthred, who, though indeed without any such benevolent intention on his own part, was the general butt of the evening. The peddler and he were closely engaged in a dispute upon the preference due to the Spanish netherstock over the black Gascoigne hose, and mine host had just winked to the guests around him, as who should say, "You will have mirth presently, my masters," when the trampling of horses was heard in the courtyard, and the hostler was loudly summoned, with a few of the newest oaths then in vogue, to add force to the invocation. Out tumbled Will Hostler, John Tapster, and all the militia of the inn, who had slunk from their posts in order to collect some scattered crumbs of the mirth which was flying about among the customers. Out into the yard sallied mine host himself also, to do fitting salutation to his new guests.

Recalling Facts

1. The fabric merchant came from
   - ☐ a. Cumnor.
   - ☐ b. Abingdon.
   - ☐ c. Gascoigne.

2. The customers gathered around the fire and
   - ☐ a. poked fun at the peddler.
   - ☐ b. quietly ate their meals.
   - ☐ c. talked over the day's events.

3. Peddlers in those days traveled by
   - ☐ a. packhorse.
   - ☐ b. wagon train.
   - ☐ c. canoe.

4. The peddler provided the people with
   - ☐ a. bottles of ale.
   - ☐ b. merriment.
   - ☐ c. new horses.

5. The general butt of the evening's jokes was
   - ☐ a. Mistress Cicely.
   - ☐ b. Master Goldthred.
   - ☐ c. Will Hostler.

Understanding the Passage

6. "Autolycus's profession" refers to
   - ☐ a. soldiers.
   - ☐ b. merchants.
   - ☐ c. stage actors.

7. The narrator does not have a very high opinion of
   - ☐ a. modern-day peddlers.
   - ☐ b. Giles Gosling.
   - ☐ c. the public room of the Black Bear.

8. A Franklin was apparently a man who
   - ☐ a. couldn't be trusted.
   - ☐ b. built fireplaces.
   - ☐ c. had some wealth.

9. The peddler and Master Goldthred did not agree on the
   - ☐ a. best kind of stocking.
   - ☐ b. quality of the food at the Black Bear.
   - ☐ c. meaning behind Miss Cicely's laugh.

10. The trampling of horses apparently meant that
    - ☐ a. the guests were leaving.
    - ☐ b. more customers were coming.
    - ☐ c. there was an emergency nearby.

13   *from* **The Death of Iván Ilyitch** *by Leo Tolstoy*

Praskovia Feódorovna blamed her husband, Iván Ilyitch, for all the misfortunes that came upon them in their new place of abode. The majority of the subjects of conversation between husband and wife, especially the education of their children, led to questions which were productive of quarrels, so that quarrels were always ready to break out. Only at rare intervals came those periods of affection which distinguish married life, but they were not of long duration. These were little islands in which they rested for a time; but then again they pushed out into the sea of secret animosity, which expressed itself by driving them farther and farther apart.

This alienation might have irritated Iván Ilyitch, if he had not considered that it was inevitable; but now he began to look upon this situation not merely as normal, but even as a way of manifesting his activity in the family. The way consisted in withdrawing as far as possible from these unpleasantnesses, or of giving them a character of innocence and respectability; and he attained this end by spending less and less time with his family; but when he was to do so, then he endeavored to secure his situation by the presence of strangers.

But Iván Ilyitch's chief resource was his office. In the world of his duties was concentrated all his interest in life. And this interest wholly absorbed him. The consciousness of his power of ruining any one whom he might wish to ruin; the importance of his position manifested outwardly when he came into court, or met his subordinates; his success with superiors and subordinates; and, above all, his skill in the conduct of affairs—and he was perfectly conscious of it—all this delighted him, and together with conversations with colleagues, dinners and whist, filled all his life. Thus, for the most part, Iván Ilyitch's life continued to flow in its even tenor as he considered that it ought to flow—pleasantly and respectably.

Thus he lived seven years longer. His eldest daughter was already sixteen years old; still another little child died; and there remained a lad, a secondary school student, the object of their wrangling. Iván Ilyitch wanted him to study the law; but Praskovia, out of spite toward him, refused to allow it. The daughter studied at home, and made good progress: the lad also was not at all backward in his studies.

Recalling Facts

1. Praskovia and Iván
   - ☐ a. often argued.
   - ☐ b. agreed on their children's education.
   - ☐ c. enjoyed traveling together.

2. Iván's most important concern was his
   - ☐ a. family.
   - ☐ b. friends.
   - ☐ c. job.

3. Iván worked in
   - ☐ a. the army.
   - ☐ b. a court.
   - ☐ c. a factory.

4. Iván's job gave him
   - ☐ a. a great deal of power.
   - ☐ b. little chance to express himself.
   - ☐ c. a small but adequate salary.

5. Iván wanted to send his son to
   - ☐ a. medical school.
   - ☐ b. law school.
   - ☐ c. military school.

Understanding the Passage

6. Iván tried to
   - ☐ a. reconcile with his wife.
   - ☐ b. get a divorce.
   - ☐ c. stay out of the house most of the time.

7. Apparently, most of the men Iván knew had
   - ☐ a. much better marriages.
   - ☐ b. marriages similar to his own.
   - ☐ c. never gotten married.

8. Iván was very
   - ☐ a. successful in his job.
   - ☐ b. close to his children.
   - ☐ c. unhappy with his parents.

9. Praskovia refused to send her son to law school to
   - ☐ a. punish him.
   - ☐ b. make her husband angry
   - ☐ c. save money.

10. Iván's children
    - ☐ a. struggled to pass their courses.
    - ☐ b. had few troubles in school.
    - ☐ c. always agreed with their mother.

I do not think that any of us who enjoyed the acquaintance of the Piper girls or the hospitality of Judge Piper, their father, ever cared for the youngest sister. Not on account of her extreme youth, for the eldest Miss Piper confessed to twenty-six—and the youth of the youngest sister was established solely, I think, by one big braid down her back. Neither was it because she was the plainest, for the beauty of the Piper girls was a recognized general distinction, and the youngest Miss Piper was not entirely devoid of the family charms. Nor was it from any lack of intelligence, nor from any defective social quality; for her precocity was astounding, and her good-humored frankness alarming. Neither do I think it could be said that a slight deafness, which might impart an embarrassing publicity to any statement—the reverse of our general feeling—that might be confided by anyone to her private ear, was a sufficient reason; for it was pointed out that she always understood everything that Tom Sparrell told her in his ordinary tone of voice. Briefly, it was very possible that Delaware—the youngest Miss Piper—did not like us.

Yet it was fondly believed by us that the other sisters failed to show that indifference to our existence shown by Miss Delaware, although the heart-burnings, misunderstandings, jealousies, hopes, and fears, and finally the chivalrous resignation with which we at last accepted the long foregone conclusion that they were not for us, and far beyond our reach, is not a part of this veracious chronicle. Enough that none of the flirtations of her elder sisters affected or were shared by the youngest Miss Piper. She moved in this heartbreaking atmosphere with sublime indifference, treating her sisters' affairs with what we considered rank simplicity or appalling frankness. Their few admirers who were weak enough to attempt to gain her mediation or confidence had reason to regret it.

"It's no kind o' use givin' me goodies," she said to a helpless suitor of Louisiana Piper's who had offered to bring her some sweets, "for I ain't got no influence with Lu, and if I don't give 'em up to her when she hears of it, she'll nag me and hate you like pizen. Unless," she added thoughtfully, "it was wintergreen lozenges; Lu can't stand them or anybody who eats them within a mile."

Recalling Facts

1. The oldest Piper sister claimed to be
   - ☐ a. twenty years old.
   - ☐ b. twenty-three years old.
   - ☐ c. twenty-six years old.

2. People recognized that the Piper sisters were
   - ☐ a. poor but respectable.
   - ☐ b. hardworking.
   - ☐ c. rather attractive.

3. Delaware was the first name of
   - ☐ a. Judge Piper.
   - ☐ b. the youngest Miss Piper.
   - ☐ c. the oldest Miss Piper.

4. The youngest Piper sister said she had no influence
   - ☐ a. with her father.
   - ☐ b. with her sister Lu.
   - ☐ c. over her suitors.

5. Lu couldn't stand
   - ☐ a. any kind of sweets.
   - ☐ b. wintergreen lozenges.
   - ☐ c. men bearing gifts.

Understanding the Passage

6. The youngest Piper sister appeared to be
   - ☐ a. bright and honest.
   - ☐ b. without many personal attributes.
   - ☐ c. moody and deceitful.

7. The youngest Piper sister was apparently
   - ☐ a. unable to hear unless one was up close.
   - ☐ b. deaf in one ear because of an accident in childhood.
   - ☐ c. able to hear the things she really wanted to hear.

8. The narrator and his friends had
   - ☐ a. no chance of attracting any Piper sister.
   - ☐ b. high hopes of marrying the younger sister.
   - ☐ c. little regard for the Piper sisters.

9. The one Piper sister that never engaged in flirtations was
   - ☐ a. Louisiana.
   - ☐ b. Virginia.
   - ☐ c. Delaware.

10. The narrator and his friends did not like the youngest Miss Piper because she
    - ☐ a. could not be trusted.
    - ☐ b. did not like them.
    - ☐ c. was young and immature.

15 *from* **The Decline and Fall of the Roman Empire** *by Edward Gibbon*

Such was the unhappy condition of the Roman emperors, that, whatever might be their conduct, their fate was commonly the same. A life of pleasure or virtue, of severity or mildness, of indolence or glory, alike led to an untimely grave; and almost every reign is closed by the same disgusting repetition of treason and murder. The death of Aurelian, however, is remarkable by its extraordinary consequences. The legions admired, lamented, and revenged their victorious chief. The artifice of his perfidious secretary was discovered and punished. The deluded conspirators attended the funeral of their injured sovereign with sincere or well-feigned contrition, and submitted to the unanimous resolution of the military order, which was signified by the following epistle: "The brave and fortunate armies to the senate and people of Rome. The crime of one man, and the error of many, have deprived us of the late emperor Aurelian. May it please you, venerable lords and fathers, to place him in the number of the gods, and to appoint a successor whom your judgment shall declare worthy of the Imperial purple! None of those whose guilt or misfortune have contributed to our loss shall ever reign over us." The Roman senators heard, without surprise, that another emperor had been assassinated in his camp; they secretly rejoiced in the fall of Aurelian; but the modest and dutiful address of the legions, when it was communicated in full assembly by the consul, diffused the most pleasing astonishment. Such honors as fear and perhaps esteem could extort they liberally poured forth on the memory of their deceased sovereign. Such acknowledgments as gratitude could inspire they returned to the faithful armies of the republic, who entertained so just a sense of the legal authority of the senate in the choice of an emperor. Yet, notwithstanding this flattering appeal, the most prudent of the assembly declined exposing their safety and dignity to the caprice of an armed multitude. The strength of the legions was, indeed, a pledge of their sincerity; but could it naturally be expected that a hasty repentance would correct the inveterate habits of fourscore years? Should the soldiers relapse into their accustomed seditions, their insolence might disgrace the majesty of the senate and prove fatal to the object of its choice. Motives like these dictated a decree by which the election of a new emperor was referred to the suffrage of the military order.

Recalling Facts

1. Almost all Roman emperors
   - ☐ a. suffered the same fate.
   - ☐ b. ruled successfully.
   - ☐ c. conducted themselves in the same way.

2. Most reigns ended with
   - ☐ a. an election.
   - ☐ b. the outbreak of widespread war.
   - ☐ c. treason and murder.

3. The conspirators
   - ☐ a. attended the funeral of Aurelian.
   - ☐ b. were rounded up and executed.
   - ☐ c. headed up the new regime.

4. The epistle proposed that Aurelian be
   - ☐ a. buried at sea.
   - ☐ b. placed with the gods.
   - ☐ c. proclaimed the bravest of Roman emperors.

5. No emperor could last long without the support of the
   - ☐ a. military.
   - ☐ b. Roman people.
   - ☐ c. both a and b.

Understanding the Passage

6. Aurelian was
   - ☐ a. condemned by his legions.
   - ☐ b. murdered by his brother.
   - ☐ c. betrayed by his secretary.

7. The conspirators appeared to be
   - ☐ a. spiteful.
   - ☐ b. remorseful.
   - ☐ c. joyful.

8. In Roman times, purple was the color of
   - ☐ a. a burial shroud.
   - ☐ b. a battle flag.
   - ☐ c. the Imperial throne.

9. Apparently, the epistle
   - ☐ a. came as a surprise to the senate.
   - ☐ b. was rejected out of hand by the senate.
   - ☐ c. was eagerly embraced by the senate.

10. The senate's attitude became one of
    - ☐ a. extreme caution.
    - ☐ b. outright hostility toward the military.
    - ☐ c. open disregard for the wishes of the legions.

from **The Spector Bridegroom** *by Washington Irving*

On the summit of one of the heights of the Odenwald, a wild and romantic tract of Upper Germany that lies not far from the confluence of the Main and the Rhine, there stood, many, many years since, the Castle of the Baron Von Landshort. It is now quite fallen to decay, and almost buried among beech trees and dark firs; above which, however, its old watchtower may still be seen struggling, like the former professor I have mentioned, to carry a high head, and look down upon a neighboring country.

The Baron was a dry branch of the great family of Katzenellenbogen, and inherited the relics of the property and all the pride of his ancestors. Though the warlike disposition of his predecessors had much impaired the family possessions, yet the Baron still endeavored to keep up some show of former state. The times were peaceable, and the German nobles, in general, had abandoned their inconvenient old castles, perched like eagles' nests among the mountains, and had built more convenient residences in the valleys; still the Baron remained proudly drawn up in his little fortress, cherishing with hereditary inveteracy all the old family feuds; so that he was on ill terms with some of his nearest neighbors, on account of disputes that had happened between their great-great-grandfathers.

The Baron had but one child, a daughter; but Nature, when she grants but one child, always compensates by making it a prodigy; and so it was with the daughter of the Baron. All the nurses, gossips, and country cousins assured her father that she had not her equal for beauty in all Germany; and who should know better than they? She had, moreover, been brought up with great care, under the superintendence of two maiden aunts, who had spent some years of their early life at one of the little German courts, and were skilled in all the branches of knowledge necessary to the education of a fine lady. Under their instructions, she became a miracle of accomplishments. By the time she was eighteen she could embroider to admiration, and had worked whole histories of the saints in tapestry with such strength of expression in their countenances that they looked like so many souls in purgatory. She could read without great difficulty, and had spelled her way through several church legends, and almost all the chivalric wonders of the Heldenbuch.

Recalling Facts

1. The castle of the Baron Von Landshort was located
   - ☐ a. on a mountain in Odenwald.
   - ☐ b. near the mouth of the Rhine.
   - ☐ c. in the middle of a city in Upper Germany.

2. The castle
   - ☐ a. is now a famous tourist attraction.
   - ☐ b. has now fallen into decay.
   - ☐ c. was never occupied.

3. The Baron's ancestors were known as
   - ☐ a. bankers.
   - ☐ b. physicians.
   - ☐ c. warriors.

4. The Baron's relations with some of his neighbors were
   - ☐ a. cold but correct.
   - ☐ b. warm and friendly.
   - ☐ c. hostile and aloof.

5. The Baron had
   - ☐ a. one daughter.
   - ☐ b. two sons.
   - ☐ c. many children.

Understanding the Passage

6. The castle
   - ☐ a. was extremely old.
   - ☐ b. had been built by the Baron's father.
   - ☐ c. had been built by the Baron himself.

7. The Baron was
   - ☐ a. well liked.
   - ☐ b. stubborn and proud.
   - ☐ c. dishonest and frugal.

8. The Baron's ancestors
   - ☐ a. were peaceful farmers
   - ☐ b. were originally from Lower Germany.
   - ☐ c. lost many possessions in the course of their battles.

9. The Baron
   - ☐ a. was a progressive leader.
   - ☐ b. wanted to live in the village.
   - ☐ c. refused to follow the lead of other nobles.

10. The Baron's daughter was
   - ☐ a. very plain.
   - ☐ b. beautiful but cruel.
   - ☐ c. lovely and talented.

from **A Foregone Conclusion** *by William Dean Howells*

Mrs. Vervain could with difficulty be got to church; but her daughter missed no service of the English ritual in the old palace where the British and American tourists assembled once a week with their guidebooks in one pocket and their prayer books in the other, and buried the tomahawk under the altar. Mr. Ferris was often sent with her, and then his thoughts, which were a young man's, wandered from the service to the beautiful girl at his side; the golden head that punctiliously bowed itself at the proper places in the liturgy; the full lips that murmured the responses; the silken lashes that swept her pale cheeks as she perused the morning lesson. He knew that the Vervains were not Episcopalians when at home, for Mrs. Vervain had told him so, and that Florida went to the English service because there was no other. He conjectured that perhaps her touch of ritualism came from mere love of any form she could make sure of.

The servants in Mrs. Vervain's lightly ordered household, with the sympathetic quickness of the Italians, learned to use him as the next friend of the family, and though they may have had their decorous surprise at his untrammeled footing, they probably excused the whole relation as a phase of that foreign eccentricity to which their nation is so amiable. If they were not able to cast the same mantle of charity over Don Ippolito's allegiance—and doubtless they had their reserves concerning such frankly familiar treatment of so dubious a character as a priest—still as a priest they stood somewhat in awe of him; they had the spontaneous loyalty of their race to the people they served, and they never intimated by a look that they found it strange when Don Ippolito freely came and went. Mrs. Vervain had quite adopted him into her family; while her daughter seemed more at ease with him than with Ferris, and treated him with a grave politeness which had something also of compassion and childlike reverence in it. Ferris observed that she was always particularly careful of his supposable sensibilities as a Roman Catholic, and that the priest was oddly indifferent to this deference, as if it would have mattered very little to him whether his church was spared or not. He had a way of lightly avoiding all phases of religion as matters of indifference.

Recalling Facts

1. Mrs. Vervain went to church
   - ☐ a. twice a week.
   - ☐ b. almost every Sunday.
   - ☐ c. rarely.

2. Miss Vervain was
   - ☐ a. a beautiful girl.
   - ☐ b. a lonely widow.
   - ☐ c. often absent from church.

3. The church service mentioned in this passage was
   - ☐ a. Roman Catholic.
   - ☐ b. Episcopalian.
   - ☐ c. Presbyterian.

4. The servants at Mrs. Vervain's house were
   - ☐ a. English.
   - ☐ b. Italian.
   - ☐ c. French.

5. Don Ippolito seemed to regard religious questions with
   - ☐ a. indifference.
   - ☐ b. great curiosity.
   - ☐ c. apparent disapproval.

Understanding the Passage

6. During the church service, Mr. Ferris's attention was focused on
   - ☐ a. Miss Vervain.
   - ☐ b. the priest.
   - ☐ c. his guidebook.

7. Florida apparently felt a great need to
   - ☐ a. converse with priests.
   - ☐ b. avoid her mother's servants.
   - ☐ c. attend church services.

8. The servants appeared to be
   - ☐ a. tolerant.
   - ☐ b. dishonest.
   - ☐ c. inattentive.

9. The servants seemed to be most suspicious of
   - ☐ a. Mr. Ferris.
   - ☐ b. Miss Vervain.
   - ☐ c. Don Ippolito.

10. Miss Vervain tried not to
    - ☐ a. offend Don Ippolito.
    - ☐ b. show her passion for Mr. Ferris.
    - ☐ c. display reverence for the priest.

Soon, with a deep sigh, Hepzibah put aside the savory volume, and inquired of Phoebe whether old Speckle, as she called one of the hens, had laid an egg the preceding day. Phoebe ran to see, but returned without the expected treasure in her hand. At that instant, however, the blast of a fish dealer's conch was heard, announcing his approach along the street. With energetic raps at the shop window, Hepzibah summoned the man in, and made purchase of what he warranted as the finest mackerel in his cart, and as fat a one as ever he felt with his finger so early in the season. Requesting Phoebe to roast some coffee—which she casually observed was the real Mocha, and so long kept that each of the small berries ought to be worth its weight in gold—the maiden lady heaped fuel into the vast receptable of the ancient fireplace in such quantity as soon to drive the lingering dusk out of the kitchen. The country girl, willing to give her utmost assistance, proposed to make an Indian cake, after her mother's peculiar method, of easy manufacture, and which she could vouch for as possessing a richness, and, if rightly prepared, a delicacy, unequalled by any other mode of breakfast cake. Hepzibah gladly assenting, the kitchen was soon the scene of savory preparation. Perchance, amid their proper element of smoke, which eddied forth from the ill-constructed chimney, the ghosts of departed cook-maids looked wonderingly on, or peeped down the great breadth of the flue, despising the simplicity of the projected meal, yet ineffectually pining to thrust their shadowy hands into each inchoate dish. The half-starved rats, at any rate, stole visibly out of their hiding places, and sat on their hind legs, snuffing the fumy atmosphere, and wistfully awaiting an opportunity to nibble.

Hepzibah had no natural turn for cookery, and, to say the truth, had fairly incurred her present meagerness by often choosing to go without her dinner rather than be attendant on the rotation of the spit, or ebullition of the pot. Her zeal over the fire, therefore, was quite an heroic test of sentiment. It was touching, and positively worthy of tears (if Phoebe, the only spectator, except the rats and ghosts aforesaid, had not been better employed than in shedding them), to see her rake out a bed of fresh and glowing coals, and proceed to broil the mackerel.

Recalling Facts

1. Old Speckle was a
   - ☐ a. conch.
   - ☐ b. fish dealer.
   - ☐ c. hen.

2. The fish dealer sold Hepzibah some
   - ☐ a. mackerel.
   - ☐ b. haddock.
   - ☐ c. flounder.

3. The coffee Phoebe roasted was real
   - ☐ a. Java.
   - ☐ b. Mocha.
   - ☐ c. Colombian.

4. The chimney was
   - ☐ a. poorly constructed.
   - ☐ b. very small.
   - ☐ c. the finest in the village.

5. The fish was to be
   - ☐ a. baked.
   - ☐ b. boiled.
   - ☐ c. broiled.

Understanding the Passage

6. Hepzibah did not like to
   - ☐ a. speak to the fish dealer.
   - ☐ b. shop for food.
   - ☐ c. cook.

7. The narrator believes that ghosts feel most comfortable
   - ☐ a. in basements.
   - ☐ b. amid smoke.
   - ☐ c. on rainy days.

8. Hepzibah lived in
   - ☐ a. a basement room.
   - ☐ b. an old house.
   - ☐ c. an attic.

9. Apparently Phoebe's mother was
   - ☐ a. named Hepzibah.
   - ☐ b. a good cook.
   - ☐ c. a fish dealer.

10. Hepzibah was
    - ☐ a. very fat.
    - ☐ b. quite thin.
    - ☐ c. spiritual.

Just before Annixter's arrival, Anne Derrick had been sitting, thoughtful, in her long chair, an open volume of poems turned down upon her lap, her glance losing itself in the immensity of Los Muertos that, from the edge of the lawn close by, unrolled itself, gigantic, toward the far southern horizon, wrinkled and serrated after the season's plowing. The earth, hitherto gray with dust, was now upturned and brown. As far as the eye could reach, it was empty of all life, bare, mournful, absolutely still; and as she looked, there seemed to her morbid imagination—diseased and disturbed with long •
brooding, sick with the monotony of repeated sensation—to be disengaged from all this immensity a sense of a vast oppression, formless, disquieting. The terror of sheer bigness grew slowly in her mind; loneliness beyond words gradually enveloped her. She was lost in all these limitless reaches of space. Had she been abandoned in mid-ocean, in an open boat, her terror could hardly have been greater. She felt vividly that certain uncongeniality which, when all is said, forever remains between humanity and the earth which supports it. She recognized the colossal indifference of nature, not hostile, even kindly and friendly, so long as the human ant swarm was •
submissive, working with it, hurrying along at its side in the mysterious march of the centuries. Let, however, the insect rebel, strive to make head against the power of this nature, and at once it became relentless, a gigantic engine, a vast power, huge, terrible; a leviathan with a heart of steel, knowing no compunction, no forgiveness, no tolerance; crushing out the human atom with soundless calm, the agony of destruction sending never a jar, never the faintest tremor through all that prodigious mechanism of wheels and cogs.

Such thoughts as these did not take shape distinctly in her mind. She •
could not have told herself exactly what it was that disquieted her. She only received the vague sensation of these things, as it were a breath of wind upon her face, confused, troublous, an indefinite sense of hostility in the air.

The sound of hoofs grinding upon the gravel of the driveway brought her to herself again, and withdrawing her gaze from the empty plain of Los Muertos, she saw young Annixter stopping his horse by the carriage steps. But the sight of him only diverted her mind to the other trouble.

Recalling Facts

1. Just before Annixter's arrival, Anne Derrick had been
   - a. reading a novel.
   - b. gazing out across the landscape.
   - c. sleeping in her long chair.

2. The fields had just been
   - a. plowed.
   - b. planted.
   - c. harvested.

3. The sheer bigness of the country made Anne feel
   - a. lonely.
   - b. jubilant.
   - c. invulnerable.

4. Anne felt in the air an indefinite sense of
   - a. fruitfulness.
   - b. warmth.
   - c. hostility.

5. Young Annixter arrived by
   - a. train.
   - b. wagon.
   - c. horse.

Understanding the Passage

6. Anne seemed to enjoy reading
   - a. magazine features.
   - b. poetry.
   - c. biographies.

7. Los Muertos appeared to be a
   - a. vast open plain.
   - b. mountain range.
   - c. deep sheltered valley.

8. Anne's feelings could best be described as
   - a. expectant and excited.
   - b. bored and frustrated.
   - c. uncomfortable and unnerved.

9. "The insect rebel" referred to the
   - a. disruptive humans.
   - b. swarming locusts.
   - c. earth itself.

10. The arrival of Annixter caused Anne to
   - a. cry out with happiness
   - b. run into the house.
   - c. think about other problems.

My grandfather's cousin—by courtesy my great-aunt—with whom we used to stay, was the mother of that aunt Leonie who, since her husband's (my uncle Octave's) death, had gradually declined to leave, first Combray, then her house in Combray, then her bedroom, and finally her bed; and who now never "came down," but lay perpetually in an indefinite condition of grief, physical exhaustion, illness, obsessions, and religious observances. Her own room looked out over the Rue Saint-Jacques, which ran a long way further to end in the Grand-Pre (as distinct from the Petit-Pre, a green space in the center of the town where three streets met) and which, monotonous and grey, with the three high steps of stone before almost every one of its doors, seemed like a deep furrow cut by some sculptor of gothic images in the very block of stone out of which he had fashioned a Calvary or a Crib. My aunt's life was now practically confined to two adjoining rooms, in one of which she would rest in the afternoon while they aired the other. They were rooms of that country order which (just as in certain climes whole tracts of air or ocean are illuminated or scented by myriads of protozoa which we cannot see) fascinate our sense of smell with the countless odors springing from their own special virtues, wisdom, habits, a whole secret system of life, invisible, superabundant and pro-foundly moral, which their atmosphere holds in solution; smells natural enough indeed, and colored by circumstances as are those of the neigh-boring countryside, but already humanized, domesticated, confined, an exquisite, skillful, limpid jelly, blending all the fruits of the season which have left the orchard for the storeroom, smells changing with the year, but plenishing, domestic smells, which compensate for the sharpness of hoar-frost with the sweet savor of warm bread, smells lazy and punctual as a village clock, roving smells, pious smells; rejoicing in a peace which brings only an increase of anxiety and in a prosiness which serves as a deep source of poetry to the stranger who passes through their midst without having lived amongst them. The air of those rooms was saturated with the fine bouquet of a silence so nourishing, so succulent that I could not enter them without a sort of greedy enjoyment, particularly on those first morn-ings, chilly still, of the Easter holidays.

Recalling Facts

1. Octave was the narrator's
   - ☐ a. uncle.
   - ☐ b. grandfather.
   - ☐ c. cousin.

2. In the end, the narrator's aunt refused to leave
   - ☐ a. Combray.
   - ☐ b. her house in Combray.
   - ☐ c. her bed.

3. The Rue Saint-Jacques was
   - ☐ a. a green space.
   - ☐ b. grey and monotonous.
   - ☐ c. decorated for the holidays.

4. Leonie's house was filled with
   - ☐ a. expensive antiques.
   - ☐ b. countless odors.
   - ☐ c. sickly relatives.

5. Leonie's condition began to decline after the death of her
   - ☐ a. only son.
   - ☐ b. beloved mother.
   - ☐ c. husband.

Understanding the Passage

6. With the passage of time, Leonie's world
   - ☐ a. constricted.
   - ☐ b. grew more complex.
   - ☐ c. became filled with joy.

7. The smells in Leonie's house
   - ☐ a. reminded the narrator of Paris.
   - ☐ b. changed with the seasons.
   - ☐ c. struck most people as repugnant.

8. During the Easter holidays, the narrator
   - ☐ a. enjoyed entering Leonie's house.
   - ☐ b. dreaded seeing Leonie.
   - ☐ c. found a nurse to stay with Leonie.

9. According to the narrator, Leonie's house smelled like
   - ☐ a. no other place in the world.
   - ☐ b. most country houses.
   - ☐ c. the ocean.

10. Apparently, the rooms of Leonie's house were usually
    - ☐ a. quiet.
    - ☐ b. warm.
    - ☐ c. dark.

The now famous Joyce-Armstrong fragment was found in the field which
is called Lower Haycock, lying one mile to the westward of the village of
Withyham, upon the Kent and Sussex border. It was on the fifteenth of
September last that an agricultural laborer, James Flynn, in the employ-
ment of Mathew Dodd, farmer, of the Chauntry Farm, Withyham, perceived
a briar pipe lying near the footpath which skirts the hedge in Lower
Haycock. A few paces farther on he picked up a pair of broken binocular
glasses. Finally, among some nettles in the ditch, he caught sight of a flat,
canvas-backed book, which proved to be a notebook with detachable
leaves, some of which had come loose and were fluttering along the base
of the hedge. These he collected, but some, including the first, were never
recovered, and leave a deplorable hiatus in this all-important statement by
Joyce-Armstrong. The notebook was taken by the laborer to his master,
who in turn showed it to Dr. J. H. Atherton, of Hartfield. This gentleman at
once recognized the need for an expert examination, and the manuscript
was forwarded to the Aero Club in London, where it now lies.

The first two pages of the manuscript are missing, and there is another
one torn away at the end of the narrative, though none of these affect the
general coherence of the story. It is conjectured that the missing opening
is concerned with the record of Mr. Joyce-Armstrong's qualifications as an
aeronaut, which can be gathered from other sources and are admitted to
be unsurpassed among the air pilots of England. For many years he has
been looked upon as among the most daring and the most intellectual of
flying men, a combination which has enabled him to both invent and test
several new devices, including the common gyroscopic attachment which
is known by his name. The main body of the manuscript is written neatly
in ink, but the last few lines are in pencil and are so ragged as to be hardly
legible—exactly, in fact, as they might be expected to appear if they were
scribbled off hurriedly from the seat of a moving aeroplane. There are, it
may be added, several stains, both on the last page and on the outside
cover, which have been pronounced by the Home Office experts to be
blood—probably human and certainly mammalian.

Recalling Facts

1. The Joyce-Armstrong fragment was found
   - ☐ a. in the wreckage of a fallen airplane.
   - ☐ b. in a field near Withyham.
   - ☐ c. on the steps of the Home Office.

2. The laborer who found the manuscript
   - ☐ a. showed it to his employer.
   - ☐ b. burned several of the pages.
   - ☐ c. buried it in a field.

3. The manuscript eventually wound up
   - ☐ a. at the Aero Club of London.
   - ☐ b. in the possession of Joyce-Armstrong's widow.
   - ☐ c. at the University of London.

4. Joyce-Armstrong was a
   - ☐ a. Chauntry Farm laborer.
   - ☐ b. college professor.
   - ☐ c. daring pilot.

5. On the cover of the manuscript, experts found
   - ☐ a. fingerprints.
   - ☐ b. traces of blood.
   - ☐ c. barely legible writing.

Understanding the Passage

6. The fact that some pages were missing from the manuscript
   - ☐ a. ruined its value.
   - ☐ b. did not alter its main thrust.
   - ☐ c. led authorities to arrest James Flynn.

7. In the field of aeronautics, Joyce-Armstrong was
   - ☐ a. considered a novice.
   - ☐ b. well respected.
   - ☐ c. virtually unknown.

8. The laborer who found the manuscript
   - ☐ a. believed it was worthless.
   - ☐ b. did not understand English.
   - ☐ c. was not qualified to assess its value.

9. The laborer tried to
   - ☐ a. keep his discovery of the manuscript a secret
   - ☐ b. recover all the pages of the manuscript.
   - ☐ c. pass the manuscript off as his own work.

10. The last lines of the manuscript were written
    - ☐ a. in haste.
    - ☐ b. by someone other than Joyce-Armstrong.
    - ☐ c. in a kind of code.

Suddenly I was attracted by Bartleby's closed desk, the key in open sight in the lock.

I mean no mischief, seek the gratification of no heartless curiosity, thought I; so I will make bold to look within. Everything was methodically arranged, the papers smoothly placed. The pigeonholes were deep, and, removing the documents, I groped into their recesses. Presently I felt something, and dragged it out. It was an old bandana handkerchief, heavy and knotted. Opening it, I saw it was a savings bank.

I now recalled all the quiet mysteries I had noted in the man. I remembered that he never spoke but to answer; that although at intervals he had considerable time to himself, yet I had never seen him reading—no, not even a newspaper; that for long periods he would stand looking out, at his window behind the screen, upon the dead brick wall; I was quite certain he never visited any refectory or eating house; while his pale face clearly indicated that he never drank beer like Turkey, or tea or coffee even, like other men; that he never went anywhere in particular that I could learn; never went out for a walk, unless indeed that was the case at present; that he had declined telling who he was, or whence he came, or whether he had any relatives in the world; that though so thin and pale, he never complained of ill health. And more than all, I remembered a certain unconscious air of pallid—how shall I call it?—of pallid haughtiness, say, or rather an austere reserve about him, which had positively awed me into my tame compliance with his eccentricities, when I had feared to ask him to do the slightest incidental thing for me, even though I might know, from his long continued motionlessness, that behind his screen he must be standing in one of those deadwall reveries of his.

Revolving all these things, and coupling them with the recently discovered fact that he made my office his constant abiding place and home, and not forgetful of his morbid moodiness; revolving all these things, a prudential feeling began to steal over me. My first emotions had been those of pure melancholy and sincerest pity; but just in proportion as the forlornness of Bartleby grew and grew to my imagination, did that same melancholy merge into fear, that pity into repulsion.

Recalling Facts

1. The key to Bartleby's desk was
   - ☐ a. on top of the desk.
   - ☐ b. hanging on a hook.
   - ☐ c. in the lock.

2. Inside one of the pigeonholes the narrator found
   - ☐ a. an old handkerchief.
   - ☐ b. a newspaper.
   - ☐ c. a will.

3. Outside Bartleby's window was
   - ☐ a. an orchard.
   - ☐ b. a brick wall.
   - ☐ c. an iron rail fence.

4. Bartleby never
   - ☐ a. asked questions of the narrator.
   - ☐ b. socialized with others.
   - ☐ c. both a and b.

5. Once he began to see Bartleby often, the narrator felt
   - ☐ a. melancholy and pity.
   - ☐ b. fear and repulsion.
   - ☐ c. awe and excitement.

Understanding the Passage

6. Bartleby can best be described as
   - ☐ a. an eccentric.
   - ☐ b. an amusing conversationalist.
   - ☐ c. a nature lover.

7. Bartleby's background was
   - ☐ a. something of a mystery.
   - ☐ b. well known to his friends.
   - ☐ c. of no concern to the narrator.

8. The narrator was
   - ☐ a. somewhat intimidated by Bartleby.
   - ☐ b. himself in poor health.
   - ☐ c. hiding his money in a handkerchief.

9. Bartleby's behavior caused the narrator to
   - ☐ a. ask him to leave his office.
   - ☐ b. grow increasingly nervous.
   - ☐ c. talk to his friends about Bartleby.

10. The narrator can best be described as
    - ☐ a. malicious.
    - ☐ b. religious.
    - ☐ c. curious.

from **Barchester Towers** *by Anthony Trollope*

The Rev. Francis Arabin, fellow of Lazarus, late professor of poetry at Oxford, and present vicar of St. Ewold, in the diocese of Barchester, must now be introduced personally to the reader. And as he will find a conspicuous place in the volume, it is desirable that he should be made to stand before the reader's eye by the aid of such portraiture as the author is able to produce.

It is to be regretted that no mental method of daguerreotype or photography has yet been discovered, by which the characters of men can be reduced to writing and put into grammatical language with an unerring precision of truthful description. How often does the novelist feel, ay, and the historian also and the biographer, that he has conceived within his mind and accurately depicted on the tablet of his brain the full character and personage of a man, and that nevertheless, when he flies to pen and ink to perpetuate the portrait, his words forsake, elude, disappoint, and play the deuce with him, till at the end of a dozen pages the man described has no more resemblance to the man conceived than the signboard at the corner of the street has to the Duke of Cambridge?

And yet such mechanical descriptive skill would hardly give more satisfaction to the reader than the skill of the photographer does to the anxious mother desirous to possess an absolute duplicate of her beloved child. The likeness is indeed true; but it is a dull, dead, unfeeling, inauspicious likeness. The face is indeed there, and those looking at it will know at once whose image it is; but the owner of the face will not be proud of the resemblance.

There is no royal road to learning; no short cut to the acquirement of any valuable art. Let photographers and daguerreotypers do what they will, and improve as they may with further skill on that which skill has already done, they will never achieve a portrait of the human face divine. Let biographers, novelists, and the rest of us groan as we may under the burdens which we so often feel too heavy for our shoulders; we must either bear them up like men, or own ourselves too weak for the work we have undertaken. There is no way of writing well and also of writing easily, especially regarding Rev. Francis Arabin.

Recalling Facts

1. Rev. Francis Arabin taught
   - ☐ a. physics.
   - ☐ b. politics.
   - ☐ c. poetry.

2. The historian and the novelist face problems similar to the
   - ☐ a. jurist.
   - ☐ b. biographer.
   - ☐ c. physician.

3. The narrator feels that the person most disappointed with any photograph is the
   - ☐ a. person photographed.
   - ☐ b. photographer.
   - ☐ c. parent of the person photographed.

4. The narrator feels the inner spirit of a person cannot be captured by a
   - ☐ a. photographer.
   - ☐ b. poet.
   - ☐ c. biographer.

5. The narrator was worried about his ability to capture
   - ☐ a. the Duke of Cambridge.
   - ☐ b. the personality of Rev. Francis Arabin.
   - ☐ c. a true likeness of his child.

Understanding the Passage

6. The narrator promised the Rev. Francis Arabin would be
   - ☐ a. a major character in the story.
   - ☐ b. an outstanding poet.
   - ☐ c. his own biographer.

7. Daguerreotype apparently was
   - ☐ a. an early form of photography.
   - ☐ b. print used in books and magazines.
   - ☐ c. proper descriptive language.

8. Photographers are able to
   - ☐ a. capture a person's true character.
   - ☐ b. reproduce a dull likeness of a person.
   - ☐ c. service their clients well.

9. Writers often feel that their writing
   - ☐ a. is a task requiring silence.
   - ☐ b. fails to describe fully a character.
   - ☐ c. creates lifelike characters.

10. The narrator viewed his task as
   - ☐ a. completely hopeless.
   - ☐ b. difficult, but worth the try
   - ☐ c. easy for a professional writer.

The atmosphere of education in which Henry Adams lived was colonial, revolutionary, almost Cromwellian, as though he were steeped, from his greatest grandmother's birth, in the odor of political crime. Resistance to something was the law of New England nature; the boy looked out on the world with the instinct of resistance; for numberless generations his predecessors had viewed the world chiefly as a thing to be reformed, filled with evil forces to be abolished, and they saw no reason to suppose that they had wholly succeeded in the abolition; the duty was unchanged. That duty implied not only resistance to evil, but hatred of it. Boys naturally look on all force as an enemy, and generally find it so, but the New Englander, whether boy or man, in his long struggle with a stingy or hostile universe, had learned also to love the pleasure of hating; his joys were few.

Politics, as a practice, whatever its professions, had always been the systematic organization of hatreds, and Massachusetts politics had been as harsh as the climate. The chief charm of New England was harshness of contrasts and extremes of sensibility, so that the pleasure of hating—oneself if no better victim offered—was not its rarest amusement; but the charm was a true and natural child of the soil, not a cultivated weed of the ancients. The violence of the contrast was real and made the strongest motive of education. The double exterior nature gave life its relative values. Winter and summer, cold and heat, town and country, force and freedom, marked two modes of life and thought, balanced like lobes of the brain. Town was winter confinement, school, rule, discipline; straight, gloomy streets, piled with six feet of snow in the middle; frosts that made the snow sing under wheels or runners; thaws when the streets became dangerous to cross; society of uncles, aunts and cousins who expected children to behave themselves, and who were not always gratified; above all else, winter represented the desire to escape and go free. Town was restraint, law, unity. Country, only seven miles away, was liberty, diversity, outlawry, the endless delight of mere sense impressions given by nature for nothing, and breathed by boys without knowing it.

Boys are wild animals, rich in the treasures of sense, but the New England boy had a wider range of emotions than boys of more equable climates.

Recalling Facts

1. The atmosphere of Henry Adams's education was both colonial and
   - ☐ a. conformist.
   - ☐ b. relaxed.
   - ☐ c. revolutionary.

2. Politics was defined as the systematic organization of
   - ☐ a. hatreds.
   - ☐ b. causes.
   - ☐ c. true believers.

3. The narrator claimed that boys naturally
   - ☐ a. hate evil.
   - ☐ b. hate all force.
   - ☐ c. both a and b.

4. According to the narrator, the country represented
   - ☐ a. unity.
   - ☐ b. law.
   - ☐ c. outlawry.

5. Country was
   - ☐ a. seven miles from Town.
   - ☐ b. seventeen miles from Town.
   - ☐ c. seventy miles from Town.

Understanding the Passage

6. New England boys were taught to view the world with
   - ☐ a. suspicion.
   - ☐ b. love.
   - ☐ c. resignation.

7. Apparently, New England in winter provided boys with
   - ☐ a. rich opportunities.
   - ☐ b. few joys.
   - ☐ c. a carefree lifestyle.

8. The narrator believed the chief virtue of New England was
   - ☐ a. partly in the contrasting climate.
   - ☐ b. its harsh democratic form of government.
   - ☐ c. the historical background of the area.

9. The narrator seemed to prefer
   - ☐ a. foreign countries.
   - ☐ b. living in the city.
   - ☐ c. country life.

10. The narrator believed that New England boys needed more
   - ☐ a. schooling.
   - ☐ b. freedom.
   - ☐ c. attention.

25 *from* **Sense and Sensibility** *by Jane Austen*

Marianne's preserver, as Margaret, with more elegance than precision, styled Willoughby, called at the cottage early the next morning to make his personal inquires. He was received by Mrs. Dashwood with more than politeness—with a kindness which Sir John Middleton's account of him and her own gratitude prompted; and everything that passed during the visit tended to assure him of the sense, elegance, mutual affection, and domestic comfort of the family to whom accident had now introduced him. Of their personal charms he had not required a second interview to be convinced.

Miss Dashwood had a delicate complexion, regular features, and a remarkably pretty figure. Marianne was still handsomer. Her form, though not so correct as her sister's, in having the advantage of height, was more striking; and her face was so lovely, that when, in the common cant of praise, she was called a beautiful girl, truth was less violently outraged than usually happens. Her skin was very brown, but, from its transparency, her complexion was uncommonly brilliant; her features were all good; her smile was sweet and attractive; and in her eyes, which were very dark, there was a spirit, an eagerness, which could hardly be seen without delight. From Willoughby their expression was at first held back, by the embarrassment which the remembrance of his assistance created. But when this passed away, where her spirits became collected—when she saw that to the perfect good breeding of the gentleman, he united frankness and vivacity, and, above all, when she heard him declare that of music and dancing he was passionately fond, she gave him such a look of approbation as secured the largest share of his discourse to herself for the rest of his stay.

It was only necessary to mention any favorite amusement to engage her to talk. She could not be silent when such points were introduced, and she had neither shyness nor reserve in their discussion. They speedily discovered that their enjoyment of dancing and music was mutual, and that it arose from a general conformity of judgment in all that related to either. Encouraged by this to a further examination of his opinions, she proceeded to question him on the subject of books; her favorite authors were brought forward and dwelt upon with so rapturous a delight, that any young man of five-and-twenty must have been insensible indeed, not to become a convert.

Recalling Facts

1. Mrs. Dashwood received Willoughby with
   - □ a. special kindness.
   - □ b. indifference.
   - □ c. apparent rudeness.

2. Marianne was
   - □ a. homelier than her sister.
   - □ b. taller than her sister.
   - □ c. ten years younger than her sister.

3. Marianne's eyes were
   - □ a. blue.
   - □ b. grey.
   - □ c. dark.

4. Willoughby claimed that he loved
   - □ a. music.
   - □ b. dancing.
   - □ c. both a and b.

5. Willoughby was
   - □ a. 22 years old.
   - □ b. 25 years old.
   - □ c. 28 years old.

Understanding the Passage

6. Apparently, Willoughby had recently
   - □ a. assisted Marianne.
   - □ b. fought with Sir John.
   - □ c. become widowed.

7. The narrator feels that when a girl is called beautiful,
   - □ a. everyone believes it.
   - □ b. it is often an exaggeration.
   - □ c. it is usually the truth.

8. At first, Marianne was embarrassed by
   - □ a. the memory of Willoughby's assistance
   - □ b. her own lack of education.
   - □ c. her plain appearance.

9. Marianne and Willoughby found they
   - □ a. disliked most popular amusements.
   - □ b. had little in common.
   - □ c. greatly enjoyed each other's company.

10. Marianne showed great enthusiasm for
    - □ a. her favorite authors.
    - □ b. hiking and camping.
    - □ c. rich foods.

When John Vincent, after waiting twelve years, married Phebe Etheridge, the whole neighborhood experienced that sense of relief and satisfaction which follows the triumph of the right. Not that the fact of a true love is ever generally recognized and respected when it is first discovered; for there is a perverse quality in American human nature which will not accept the existence of any fine, unselfish passion until it has been tested and established beyond chance. There were two views of the case when John Vincent's love for Phebe, and old Reuben Etheridge's hard prohibition of the match, first became known to the community. The girls and boys ● ranged themselves on the side of the lovers, but a large majority of the older men and a few of the younger supported the tyrannical father.

Reuben Etheridge was rich and, in addition to what his daughter would naturally inherit from him, she already possessed more than her lover, at the time of their betrothal. This, in the eyes of one class, was a sufficient reason for the father's hostility. When low natures live (as they almost invariably do) wholly in the present, they neither take tenderness from the past nor warning from the possibilities of the future. It is the exceptional ● men and women who remember their youth. So these lovers received a nearly equal amount of sympathy and condemnation; and only slowly, partly through their quiet fidelity and patience, and partly through the improvement in John Vincent's worldly circumstances, was the balance changed. Old Reuben remained an unflinching despot to the last: if any relenting softness touched his heart, he sternly concealed it; and such inference as could be drawn from the fact that he, certainly knowing what would follow his death, bequeathed his daughter her proper share of his ● goods, was all that could be taken for consent.

They were married: John, a grave man in middle age, weather-beaten and worn by years of hard work and self-denial, yet not beyond the restoration of the milder second youth; and Phebe, a sad, weary woman, whose warmth of longing had been exhausted, from whom youth and its uncalculating surrenders of hope and feeling had gone forever. They began their wedded life under the shadow of the death out of which it grew, and when they united their divided homes, it seemed that a separated husband and wife had come together again.

Recalling Facts

1. John Vincent's marriage to Phebe was most resisted by
   - ☐ a. the neighbors.
   - ☐ b. Reuben Etheridge.
   - ☐ c. their young friends.

2. Reuben won support from
   - ☐ a. the local boys and girls.
   - ☐ b. John and Phebe.
   - ☐ c. the majority of older men.

3. Between the betrothal and the wedding, John's wealth
   - ☐ a. decreased.
   - ☐ b. never changed.
   - ☐ c. increased.

4. At the time of the wedding, John was
   - ☐ a. a grave man of middle age.
   - ☐ b. an unflinching despot.
   - ☐ c. a young and happy man.

5. At the time of the wedding, Phebe was a
   - ☐ a. cheerful, optimistic woman.
   - ☐ b. sad, weary woman.
   - ☐ c. tender, unsophisticated child.

Understanding the Passage

6. In the end, the community
   - ☐ a. opposed the marriage.
   - ☐ b. was still split over the marriage.
   - ☐ c. supported the marriage.

7. The narrator felt that Americans did not accept the notion of
   - ☐ a. love at first sight.
   - ☐ b. true love after marriage.
   - ☐ c. passion among ordinary people.

8. The people who supported Reuben thought that
   - ☐ a. a husband should have more money than his wife
   - ☐ b. true love conquers all difficulties.
   - ☐ c. John and Phebe were too young to marry.

9. John managed to
   - ☐ a. alienate more and more people.
   - ☐ b. soften Reuben's resistance.
   - ☐ c. win the support of more and more people.

10. For Phebe, the marriage came
    - ☐ a. too early.
    - ☐ b. at the perfect time.
    - ☐ c. too late.

The pulpit, rising ten or twelve feet high, against the rear wall, was backed by a significant mural painting, in oil—showing its bold lines through the subdued light of the building—of a stormy sea, the waves high rolling, and amid them an old-fashioned ship, all bent over, driving through the gale, and in great peril—a vivid and effectual piece of limning, not intended for the criticism of artists (although I believe it had merit even from that standpoint,) but for its effect upon the congregation, and what it would convey to them.

Father Taylor was a moderate sized man, indeed almost small, well advanced in years, but alert, with mild blue or gray eyes, and good presence and voice. Soon as he opened his mouth I ceased to pay any attention to church or audience, or pictures or lights and shades; a far more potent charm entirely swayed me. In the course of the sermon, (there was no sign of any manuscript, or reading from notes) some of the parts would be in the highest degree majestic and picturesque. Colloquial in a severe sense, it often leaned to Biblical and oriental forms. Especially were all allusions to ships and the ocean and sailors' lives, of unrivaled power and lifelikeness. Sometimes there were passages of fine language and composition, even from the purist's point of view. A few arguments, and of the best, but always brief and simple; one realized what grip there might have been in such words-of-mouth talk as that of Socrates and Epictetus. I should say, of any of these discourses, that the old Demosthenean rule and requirement of "action, action, action," first in its inward and then (very moderate and restrained) its outward sense, was the quality that had leading fulfillment.

I remember I felt the deepest impression from the old man's prayers, which invariably affected me to tears. Never, on similar or any other occasions, have I heard such impassioned pleading—such human-harassing reproach (like Hamlet to his mother, in the closet)—such probing to the very depths of that latent conscience and remorse which probably lie somewhere in the background of every life, every soul. For when Father Taylor preached or prayed, the rhetoric and art, the mere words, (which usually play such a big part) seemed altogether to disappear, and the *live feeling* advanced upon you and seized you with a power before unknown.

Recalling Facts

1. The oil painting behind the pulpit showed
   - □ a. sun and clouds.
   - □ b. a stormy sea.
   - □ c. mountains during autumn.

2. Father Taylor was
   - □ a. young.
   - □ b. middle aged.
   - □ c. elderly.

3. The narrator was most impressed by
   - □ a. Father Taylor's sermon.
   - □ b. the light coming through the windows.
   - □ c. the majesty of the church.

4. Father Taylor relied heavily on allusions about
   - □ a. the seasons.
   - □ b. the weather.
   - □ c. ships.

5. To the narrator, the words of Father Taylor seemed
   - □ a. inappropriate.
   - □ b. to disappear.
   - □ c. too colloquial.

Understanding the Passage

6. The main function of the oil painting was to
   - □ a. impress the congregation.
   - □ b. decorate the church.
   - □ c. invite critical analysis.

7. The narrator
   - □ a. rarely went to church.
   - □ b. paid close attention to the sermon.
   - □ c. couldn't take his eyes off the oil painting.

8. Father Taylor
   - □ a. preached slowly and quietly.
   - □ b. read from prepared notes.
   - □ c. spoke from the heart.

9. Socrates and Epictetus were great
   - □ a. ministers.
   - □ b. painters.
   - □ c. speakers.

10. Father Taylor's sermon left the narrator
    - □ a. emotionally drained.
    - □ b. depressed and remorseful.
    - □ c. uninspired by the clever rhetoric.

The Countess Gemini was often extraordinarily bored—bored, in her own phrase, to extinction. She had not been extinguished, however, and she struggled bravely enough with her destiny, which had been to marry an unaccommodating Florentine who insisted upon living in his native town, where he enjoyed such consideration as might attach to a gentleman whose talent for losing at cards had not the merit of being incidental to an obliging disposition. The Count Gemini was not liked even by those who won money from him; and he bore a name which, having a measurable value in Florence, was, like the local coin of the old Italian states, without currency in other parts of the peninsula. In Rome he was simply a very dull Florentine, and it is not remarkable that he should not have cared to pay frequent visits to a place where, to carry it off, his dullness needed more explanation than was convenient. The Countess lived with her eyes upon Rome, and it was the constant grievance of her existence that she had not a habitation there. She was positively ashamed to say how seldom she had been allowed to visit that city; it scarcely made the matter better that there were other members of the Florentine nobility who never had been there at all. She went whenever she could; that was all she could say—or rather not all, but all she said she could say. Actually she had much more to say about it, and had often set forth the reasons why she hated Florence and wished to end her days in the shadow of Saint Peter's. They are reasons, however, that do not closely concern us, and were usually summed up in the declaration that Rome, in short, was the Eternal City and that Florence was simply a pretty little place like any other. The Countess apparently needed to connect the idea of eternity with her amusements. She was convinced that society was infinitely more interesting in Rome, where you met celebrities all winter at evening parties. At Florence there were no celebrities; not at least that one had ever heard of. Since her brother's marriage her impatience had greatly increased; she was so certain his wife had a more brilliant life than herself. She was not so intellectual as Isabel, but she was intellectual enough to do justice to Rome.

Recalling Facts

1. The Countess Gemini was
   - ☐ a. sickly.
   - ☐ b. shy.
   - ☐ c. bored.

2. The Count Gemini was not
   - ☐ a. a good card player.
   - ☐ b. well liked.
   - ☐ c. both a and b.

3. In Rome, the Count was considered
   - ☐ a. vulgar.
   - ☐ b. dull.
   - ☐ c. brilliant.

4. Some members of the Florentine nobility had never
   - ☐ a. been to Rome.
   - ☐ b. learned to dance.
   - ☐ c. seen an opera.

5. The Countess Gemini wanted desperately to visit
   - ☐ a. the Eternal City.
   - ☐ b. all the old Italian states.
   - ☐ c. England.

Understanding the Passage

6. The Count and the Countess had different views of
   - ☐ a. gambling.
   - ☐ b. Florence.
   - ☐ c. the Count's brother.

7. The Countess was jealous of
   - ☐ a. her husband.
   - ☐ b. the rest of the Florence nobility.
   - ☐ c. Isabel.

8. The Countess could best be described as
   - ☐ a. discontent.
   - ☐ b. dishonest.
   - ☐ c. disbelieving.

9. The Count did not have
   - ☐ a. any money.
   - ☐ b. much fun in Rome.
   - ☐ c. any use for children.

10. The Countess believed she could
    - ☐ a. appreciate what Rome had to offer.
    - ☐ b. become a celebrity in Rome.
    - ☐ c. join her brother's family in Rome.

The Circus at Antioch stood on the south bank of the river, nearly opposite the island, differing in no respect from the plan of such buildings in general.

In the purest sense, the games were a gift to the public, consequently everybody was free to attend; and, vast as the holding capacity of the structure was, so fearful was the people, on this occasion, lest there should not be room for them, that, early the day before the opening of the exhibition, they took up all vacant spaces in the vicinity, where their temporary shelter suggested an army in waiting.

At midnight the entrances were thrown wide, and the rabble, surging in, occupied the quarters assigned to them from which nothing less than an earthquake could have dislodged them. They dozed the night away on the benches, and breakfasted there; and there the close of the exercises found them, patient and sight hungry as in the beginning.

The better people, their seats secured, began moving towards the Circus about the first hour of the morning, the noble and very rich among them distinguished by litters and retinues of liveried servants.

By the second hour, the efflux from the city was a stream unbroken and innumerable.

Exactly as the pointer of the official dial up in the citadel pointed the second hour half gone, the legion, in full panoply, and with all its standards on exhibit, descended from Mount Sulpius; and when the rear of the last cohort disappeared in the bridge, Antioch was literally abandoned—not that the Circus could hold the multitude, but that a multitude was gone out to it, nevertheless.

A great concourse on the river shore witnessed the consul come over from the island in a barge of state. As the great man landed, and was received by the legion, the martial show for one brief moment transcended the attraction of the Circus.

At the third hour, the audience, if such it may be termed, was assembled; at last, a flourish of trumpets called for silence, and instantly the gaze of over a hundred thousand persons was directed towards a pile forming the eastern section of the building.

There was a basement first, broken in the middle by a broad arched passage, called the Porto Pompae, over which, on an elevated tribunal magnificently decorated with insignia and legionary standards, the consul sat in the place of honor.

Recalling Facts

1. Admission to the Circus was
   - ☐ a. free.
   - ☐ b. affordable by the rabble.
   - ☐ c. only for the rich.

2. The first people in their seats were the
   - ☐ a. poor.
   - ☐ b. middle class.
   - ☐ c. rich.

3. Almost all the people left
   - ☐ a. the Circus.
   - ☐ b. the citadel.
   - ☐ c. Antioch.

4. The great man's title was
   - ☐ a. consul.
   - ☐ b. lord.
   - ☐ c. governor.

5. The Porto Pompae was
   - ☐ a. a ticket window.
   - ☐ b. the gate to Antioch.
   - ☐ c. a broad passage at the Circus.

Understanding the Passage

6. The games were apparently
   - ☐ a. an everyday attraction.
   - ☐ b. a rare event.
   - ☐ c. designed for the rich only.

7. The very rich people
   - ☐ a. were uninterested in the Circus.
   - ☐ b. were carried to the games.
   - ☐ c. arrived after the games began.

8. The Circus was located
   - ☐ a. in Antioch.
   - ☐ b. outside the city.
   - ☐ c. on an island.

9. When the trumpets sounded people were
   - ☐ a. too fascinated by the Circus to notice.
   - ☐ b. trying to get back to their seats.
   - ☐ c. instantly silent and attentive.

10. The mood of the people at the Circus could best be described as
   - ☐ a. reserved.
   - ☐ b. anticipatory.
   - ☐ c. inflammatory.

General Ople was the hero to champion a lady whose airs of haughtiness caused her to be somewhat backbitten. He assured everybody that Lady Camper was much misunderstood; she was a remarkable woman; she was an affable and highly intelligent lady. Building up her attributes on a splendid climax, he declared she was pious, charitable, witty, and really an extraordinary artist. He laid particular stress on her artistic qualities, describing her power with the brush, her watercolor sketches, and also some immensely clever caricatures. As he talked of no one else, his friends heard enough of Lady Camper, who was anything but a favorite. The Pollingtons, the Wilders, the Wardens, the Baerens, the Goslings, and others of his acquaintance, talked of Lady Camper and General Ople rather maliciously. They were all City people, and they admired the General, but mourned that he should so abjectly have fallen at the feet of a lady as red with rouge as a railway bill; his not seeing it showed the state he was in. The sister of Mrs. Pollington, an amiable widow, relict of a large City warehouse, was chilled by a falling off in his attentions; his apology for not appearing at garden parties was that he was engaged to wait on Lady Camper.

And at one time, her not condescending to exchange visits with the obsequious General was a topic fertile in irony. But she did condescend.

Lady Camper came to his gate unexpectedly, rang the bell, and was let in like an ordinary visitor. It happened that the General was gardening— not the pretty occupation of pruning, he was digging—and of necessity his coat was off, and he was hot, dusty, unpresentable. From adoring earth as the mother of roses, you may pass into a lady's presence without purification; you cannot (or so the General thought) when you are caught in the act of adoring the mother of cabbages. And though he himself loved the cabbage equally with the rose, in his heart respected the vegetable yet more than he esteemed the flower, for he gloried in his kitchen garden, this was not a secret for the world to know, and he almost heeled over on his beam ends when word was brought of the extreme honor Lady Camper had done him. He worked his arms hurriedly into his fatigue jacket, trusting to spend a couple of minutes on his adornment.

Recalling Facts

1. General Ople tried to convince people that Lady Camper was
   - ☐ a. backbitten.
   - ☐ b. haughty.
   - ☐ c. misunderstood.

2. General Ople claimed that Lady Camper was really an exceptional
   - ☐ a. artist.
   - ☐ b. writer.
   - ☐ c. singer.

3. The Pollingtons, the Goslings, and the Wardens spoke of Lady Camper
   - ☐ a. tenderly.
   - ☐ b. maliciously.
   - ☐ c. reluctantly.

4. General Ople had stopped seeing
   - ☐ a. Mrs. Pollington's sister.
   - ☐ b. Mrs. Pollington.
   - ☐ c. Mrs. Wilder.

5. When Lady Camper called on General Ople, he was
   - ☐ a. gardening.
   - ☐ b. painting.
   - ☐ c. sleeping.

Understanding the Passage

6. Lady Camper appeared to have
   - ☐ a. no real talents.
   - ☐ b. many enemies.
   - ☐ c. an agreeable appearance.

7. General Ople felt it was necessary to
   - ☐ a. teach Lady Camper social graces.
   - ☐ b. ask Lady Camper to be more charitable.
   - ☐ c. defend Lady Camper in public.

8. Apparently, Lady Camper
   - ☐ a. wore too much rouge.
   - ☐ b. enjoyed drawing caricatures.
   - ☐ c. both a and b.

9. The City people thought that General Ople was
   - ☐ a. fooling himself.
   - ☐ b. right in not attending the garden parties.
   - ☐ c. much too condescending.

10. General Ople thought that Lady Camper would
    - ☐ a. appreciate his fine cabbage.
    - ☐ b. be offended to see him grimy and unkempt.
    - ☐ c. enjoy seeing a man digging in his garden .

The trees of many acres had been felled, and the glow of a mild summer's evening had fallen on the clearing. A short distance from the place where Duncan stood, the stream had seemingly expanded into a little lake, covering most of the low land, from mountain to mountain. The water fell out of this wide basin, in a cataract so regular and gentle, that it appeared rather to be the work of human hands than fashioned by nature. A hundred earthen dwellings stood on the margin of the lake, and even in its water, as though the latter had overflowed its usual banks. Their rounded roofs, admirably molded for defense against the weather, denoted more of industry and foresight than the natives were wont to bestow on their regular habitations, much less on those they occupied for the temporary purposes of hunting and war. In short, the whole village or town, whichever it might be termed, possessed more of method and neatness of execution than the white men had been accustomed to believe belonged ordinarily to the Indian habits. It appeared, however, to be deserted. At least, so thought Duncan for many minutes; but, at length, he fancied he discovered several human forms advancing towards him on all fours, and apparently dragging in their train some heavy, and as he was quick to apprehend, some formidable engine. Just then a few dark looking heads gleamed out of the dwellings, and the place seemed suddenly alive with beings which, however, glided from cover to cover so swiftly as to allow no opportunity of examining their humors or pursuits. Alarmed at these suspicious and inexplicable movements, he was about to attempt the signal of the crows, when the rustling of leaves at hand drew his eyes in another direction.

The young man started and recoiled a few paces instinctively, when he found himself within a hundred yards of a stranger Indian. Recovering his recollection on the instant, instead of sounding an alarm, which might prove fatal to himself, he remained stationary, an attentive observer of the other's motions.

An instant of calm observation served to assure Duncan that he was undiscovered. The native, like himself, seemed occupied in considering the low dwellings of the village, and the stolen movements of its inhabitants. It was impossible to discover the expression of his features, through the mask of paint under which they were concealed.

Recalling Facts

1. The dwellings Duncan saw sat at the edge of a
   - ☐ a. lake.
   - ☐ b. cliff.
   - ☐ c. field.

2. At first, the dwellings appeared to be
   - ☐ a. the tribal headquarters.
   - ☐ b. populated only by women and children.
   - ☐ c. entirely deserted.

3. Duncan was surprised that the dwellings were
   - ☐ a. so neat and well built.
   - ☐ b. made out of dirt.
   - ☐ c. situated so close together.

4. The Indians Duncan saw were dragging
   - ☐ a. large logs.
   - ☐ b. a formidable engine.
   - ☐ c. dozens of prisoners.

5. The lone Indian standing near Duncan was
   - ☐ a. watching the activities in the village.
   - ☐ b. wearing a mask of paint.
   - ☐ c. both a and b.

Understanding the Passage

6. Duncan was a
   - ☐ a. member of the Crow tribe.
   - ☐ b. stranger to the Indians.
   - ☐ c. friend of the Indians.

7. White men did not think Indians possessed much skill as
   - ☐ a. builders.
   - ☐ b. warriors.
   - ☐ c. farmers.

8. Duncan did not want the Indians to
   - ☐ a. leave.
   - ☐ b. see him.
   - ☐ c. riot.

9. Duncan decided not to sound an alarm because it might
   - ☐ a. scare the Indians.
   - ☐ b. put him in danger.
   - ☐ c. not be heard.

10. It only took Duncan a moment to realize that he
    - ☐ a. had not been seen.
    - ☐ b. was about to be killed.
    - ☐ c. was lost.

J. Abingdon Smith, III, was still a young man, thin of hair, nearsighted, endowed with sufficient intelligence to enable him to turn over his inherited fortune, legitimately increased, to any heir he might have if he should ever marry. Had he resembled Smith the first, or Smith the second, he would have done this as a matter of family routine—married the sort of girl that generations of Smiths found inoffensive enough to marry; produced one heir, and, when the proper time arrived, would have in his turn decorously and formally faded heavenward—leaving a J. Abingdon Smith, IV, to follow his example.

But Smith had inherited from his mother a thin but deep streak of romantic sentiment. This vein ran clean through him, and might have manifested itself in almost any form along the line of least resistance, had it not been half imbedded in a stratum of negative platitudes inherited from his emotionless father.

As he stood in his shabby clothes, near the new Hall of Records, waiting for a Fourth Avenue car, a slender, blue-eyed girl, passing, looked up at him with such a frank, sweet gaze that he missed his next breath and then made up for it by breathing twice too quickly. He had an idea that he had seen her before, but finally decided he hadn't.

To be loved for himself alone was one of his impractical ideas, born of the maternal sentimental streak; but, for years, the famous Smith fortune, its enormous holdings in realty, the doings of the Smiths, their shrewd sales, purchases, leases, improvements, their movements, their personal affairs, their photographed features had been common property and an unfailing source of news for the press; and he knew perfectly well that, however honest and theoretically disinterested a girl might be, the courtship of a J. Abingdon Smith, of whatever vintage, could not help representing a bunch of figures that no human being in shape of a female biped could avoid seeing, no matter how tightly she closed her innocent eyes. Thinking of these things, he calmly encountered the curious eyes of the conductor as he boarded a crowded car.

The blue-eyed girl also got in, but Smith, on the back platform, did not see her.

"That fellow," said the conductor to the gripman, as he swung off the front platform after collecting a fare, "is a ringer for J. Abingdon Smith, the millionaire."

Recalling Facts

1. Smith was
   - ☐ a. wealthy.
   - ☐ b. not very bright.
   - ☐ c. both a and b.

2. If Smith behaved like his father and grandfather he would have
   - ☐ a. produced one heir.
   - ☐ b. married several times.
   - ☐ c. become a gambler.

3. Smith inherited from his mother a deep streak of
   - ☐ a. all-consuming greed.
   - ☐ b. romantic sentiment.
   - ☐ c. inate jealousy.

4. Smith's father lacked
   - ☐ a. intelligence.
   - ☐ b. money.
   - ☐ c. emotion.

5. The Smith fortune was made in
   - ☐ a. oil.
   - ☐ b. steel production.
   - ☐ c. real estate.

Understanding the Passage

6. Up until now, Smith had not
   - ☐ a. wanted to get married.
   - ☐ b. wanted to leave his money to anyone.
   - ☐ c. followed the Smith family tradition.

7. Smith could easily have
   - ☐ a. dressed in nicer clothes.
   - ☐ b. been overlooked by the press.
   - ☐ c. had opportunities for anonymity.

8. Smith's wealth was a handicap in finding a
   - ☐ a. private place to live.
   - ☐ b. woman who really loved him.
   - ☐ c. spot on commuter trains.

9. The conductor
   - ☐ a. did not think Smith was the real J. Abingdon Smith
   - ☐ b. thought Smith should marry the blue-eyed girl.
   - ☐ c. disliked Smith immediately.

10. Smith was attracted to
   - ☐ a. women who did not recognize him.
   - ☐ b. rich women.
   - ☐ c. the blue-eyed girl.

from **The Life and Adventures of Nicholas Nickleby** *by Charles Dickens*

After five years, when Mrs. Nickleby had presented her husband with a couple of sons, and that embarrassed gentleman, impressed with the necessity of making some provision for his family, was seriously revolving in his mind a little commercial speculation of insuring his life next quarter day, and then falling from the top of the Monument by accident, there came one morning, by the general post, a black bordered letter to inform him how his uncle, Mr. Ralph Nickleby, was dead, and had left him the bulk of his little property, amounting in all to five thousand pounds sterling.

As the deceased had taken no further notice of his nephew in his lifetime, than sending to his eldest boy (who had been christened after him, on desperate speculation) a silver spoon in a morocco case, which as he had not too much to eat with it, seemed a kind of satire upon his having been born without that useful article of plate in his mouth, Mr. Godfrey Nickleby could at first scarcely believe the tidings thus conveyed to him. On further examination, however, they turned out to be strictly correct. The amiable old gentleman, it seemed, had intended to leave the whole to the Royal Humane Society, and had indeed executed a will to that effect; but the Institution having been unfortunate enough, a few months before, to save the life of a poor relation to whom he paid a weekly allowance of three shillings and sixpence, he had in a fit of very natural exasperation, revoked the bequest, and left it all to Mr. Godfrey Nickleby; with a special mention of his indignation, not only against the society for saving the poor relation's life, but against the poor relation also, for allowing himself to be saved.

With a portion of this property Mr. Godfrey Nickleby purchased a small farm near Dawlish, whither he retired with his wife and two children, to live upon the best interest he could get for the rest of his money, and the little produce he could raise from his land. The two prospered so well together that, when he died, some fifteen years after this period, and some five after his wife, he was enabled to leave to his eldest son, Ralph, three thousand pounds in cash, and to his youngest son, Nicholas, one thousand and the farm, which is about the size of Russell Square.

Recalling Facts

1. Mr. and Mrs. Nickleby had
   - ☐ a. two boys.
   - ☐ b. three boys.
   - ☐ c. a boy and a girl.

2. Mr. Ralph Nickleby left his money to his
   - ☐ a. son.
   - ☐ b. grandson.
   - ☐ c. nephew.

3. Mr. Ralph Nickleby was upset with
   - ☐ a. Mr. Godfrey Nickleby.
   - ☐ b. the Royal Humane Society.
   - ☐ c. the children of Godfrey Nickleby.

4. With his new wealth, Mr. Godfrey Nickleby bought a
   - ☐ a. store.
   - ☐ b. boat.
   - ☐ c. farm.

5. Mrs. Nickleby died
   - ☐ a. five years before her husband.
   - ☐ b. ten years before her husband.
   - ☐ c. ten years after her husband.

Understanding the Passage

6. Before the letter arrived, Mr. Nickleby was
   - ☐ a. a wealthy man.
   - ☐ b. thinking of moving.
   - ☐ c. contemplating suicide.

7. In this passage, a silver spoon is a symbol of
   - ☐ a. a generous relative.
   - ☐ b. wealth.
   - ☐ c. talent.

8. Mr. Godfrey Nickleby's good fortune came
   - ☐ a. as a surprise.
   - ☐ b. with a farm.
   - ☐ c. with a silver spoon.

9. Mr. Ralph Nickleby was a man of
   - ☐ a. strong beliefs.
   - ☐ b. weak resolve.
   - ☐ c. forgiving nature.

10. After he became wealthy, Mr Godfrey Nickleby
    - ☐ a. lost the money gambling.
    - ☐ b. enjoyed a more prosperous life.
    - ☐ c. became ill and died untimely.

from Letter to
Mrs. Catherine Gordon Byron *by Lord Byron*

Dear Mother, I have been so much occupied since my departure from England that till I could address you at length, I have forborn writing altogether. As I have now passed through Portugal & a considerable part of Spain, & have leisure at this place I shall endeavor to give you a short detail of my movements. We sailed from Falmouth on the 2d. of July, reached Lisbon after a very favorable passage of four days and a half, and took up our abode for a time in that city. It has been often described without being worthy of description, for, except the view from the Tagus which is beautiful, and some fine churches & convents it contains little but filthy streets & more filthy inhabitants. To make amends for this the village of Cintra about fifteen miles from the capitol is perhaps in every respect the most delightful in Europe; it contains beauties of every description natural & artificial, palaces and gardens rising in the midst of rocks, cataracts, and precipices, convents on stupendous heights, a distant view of the sea and the Tagus, and besides (though that is a secondary consideration) is remarkable as the scene of Sir Hew Dalrymple's convention. It unites in itself all the wildness of the Western Highlands with the verdure of the South of France. Near this place about 10 miles to the right is the palace of Mafra, the boast of Portugal, as it might be of any country, in point of magnificence without elegance; there is a convent annexed, the monks who possess large revenues are courteous enough, & understand Latin, so that we had a long conversation, they have a large library & asked me if the *English* had *any books* in their country. I sent my baggage by sea to Gibraltar, and traveled on horseback from Aldea Gallega (the first stage from Lisbon which is only accessible by water) to Seville (one of the most famous cities in Spain where the Government called the Junta is now held). The distance to Seville is nearly four hundred miles & to Cadiz about 90 further towards the Coast. I had orders from the Government & every possible accommodation on the road, as an English nobleman in an English uniform is a very respectable personage in Spain at present. The horses are remarkably good, and the roads very far superior to the best British roads.

Recalling Facts

1. The sail from Falmouth to Lisbon
   - ☐ a. lasted four weeks.
   - ☐ b. was very pleasant.
   - ☐ c. was marred by a huge storm.

2. The narrator had a low opinion of
   - ☐ a. Lisbon.
   - ☐ b. Falmouth.
   - ☐ c. Spain.

3. The narrator thought that the most delightful village in Europe was
   - ☐ a. Tagus.
   - ☐ b. Cintra.
   - ☐ c. Mafra.

4. The narrator traveled from Aldea Gallega to Seville
   - ☐ a. by boat.
   - ☐ b. by stagecoach.
   - ☐ c. on horseback.

5. Spanish roads were
   - ☐ a. vastly inferior to British roads.
   - ☐ b. just as good as British roads.
   - ☐ c. far superior to British roads.

Understanding the Passage

6. The narrator did not like to write
   - ☐ a. long letters.
   - ☐ b. brief letters.
   - ☐ c. any letters.

7. The narrator's impression of Portugal was
   - ☐ a. one of mixed feelings.
   - ☐ b. favorable in all respects.
   - ☐ c. one of bitter disappointment.

8. The narrator spent a long time
   - ☐ a. walking the streets of Lisbon.
   - ☐ b. talking to the monks at Mafra.
   - ☐ c. reading the library's collection of English books.

9. The narrator was in the midst of
   - ☐ a. writing a novel.
   - ☐ b. a military campaign.
   - ☐ c. a long trip.

10. The narrator had apparently
    - ☐ a. never been to Europe before.
    - ☐ b. traveled extensively in Europe.
    - ☐ c. recently married a European woman.

I fell ill soon after the Christmas holidays, and was taken to our military hospital. It was a long, one-storied building, painted yellow, which stood by itself half a verst from the prison, in the midst of a very large courtyard, surrounded by the outhouses, and two or three cottages where the medical officers lived. The wards were all in the principal building. There were several of them, but only two were allotted to the convicts, and were consequently much crowded, especially in summertime when temporary beds had often to be erected and squeezed in somehow or other between the others. A great number of our patients were military prisoners who were awaiting their trial, and soldiers from the so-called reformatory battalion—a curious institution, where soldiers whose behavior has been unsatisfactory, or who have committed some trifling breach of discipline, are sent for two years or more, and which they leave as professed criminals. A convict who wished to be admitted into the hospital reported himself in the morning to the sergeant at arms, who put down his name in a book, and sent him with the book and accompanied by an escort to the field hospital, where the men who have applied to see the doctor are examined by him, and, if they are really ill, have their names put down on the hospital list.

I went to the hospital about 2 P.M., when all the other convicts had gone to their afternoon work. The patient generally took with him all the ready money he had, a large piece of bread—as neither dinner nor supper is provided for him on the day of his entering the hospital—a small pipe, a tobacco pouch and tinderbox, the latter articles being carefully hidden away in his boots.

I must confess that I entered the hospital yard not without a certain feeling of curiosity, as this side of convict life was practically unknown to me.

The day was warm and dull—one of those days when a building like a hospital is apt to appear more dreary and official looking than usual. We walked into a kind of reception room, where two other convicts were already waiting with their escorts. On one side of the room stood two tin baths. After some time had elapsed the male nurse made his appearance at last, stared at us haughtily, and then went off lazily to report us to the doctor.

Recalling Facts

1. The military hospital was located in the middle of a
   - ☐ a. labor camp.
   - ☐ b. large city.
   - ☐ c. large courtyard.

2. The convicts' hospital wards were often
   - ☐ a. somewhat empty.
   - ☐ b. terribly crowded.
   - ☐ c. used by neighboring city hospitals.

3. A soldier who broke a small rule might be sent to
   - ☐ a. the reformatory battalion.
   - ☐ b. his commanding officer.
   - ☐ c. a prison in Siberia.

4. On the first day in the hospital, a patient was
   - ☐ a. not fed.
   - ☐ b. forced to bathe.
   - ☐ c. denied the right to smoke.

5. The reception room contained
   - ☐ a. two tin baths.
   - ☐ b. no benches for sitting.
   - ☐ c. armed guards.

Understanding the Passage

6. Military discipline was
   - ☐ a. almost nonexistent.
   - ☐ b. relatively lax.
   - ☐ c. very harsh.

7. Two years in a reformatory battalion made men
   - ☐ a. want to be better citizens.
   - ☐ b. forget their families.
   - ☐ c. become hardened criminals.

8. Apparently, some convicts would
   - ☐ a. fake illness.
   - ☐ b. skip work assignments.
   - ☐ c. give a false name to the doctor.

9. Tobacco was
   - ☐ a. readily available.
   - ☐ b. surreptitiously used by sick convicts.
   - ☐ c. used to pay doctors.

10. If declared healthy by the doctor, a convict had to
    - ☐ a. go back to work.
    - ☐ b. endure a flogging.
    - ☐ c. serve extra time.

Was it ambition—real ambition—or was it mere restlessness that made Mrs. Lightfoot Lee so bitter against New York and Philadelphia, Baltimore and Boston, American life in general and all life in particular? What did she want? Not social position, for she herself was an eminently respectable Philadelphian by birth; her father a famous clergyman; and her husband had been equally irreproachable, a descendant of one branch of the Virginia Lees, which had drifted to New York in search of fortune, and had found it, or enough of it to keep the young man there. His widow had her own place in society which no one disputed. Though not brighter than her neighbors, the world persisted in classing her among clever women; she had wealth, or at least enough of it to give her all that money can give by way of pleasure to a sensible woman in an American city; she had her house and her carriage; she dressed well; her table was good, and her furniture was never allowed to fall behind the latest standard of decorative art. She had traveled in Europe, and after several visits, covering some years of time, had returned home, carrying in one hand, as it were, a green grey landscape, a remarkably pleasing specimen of Corot, and in the other some bales of Persian and Syrian rugs and embroideries, Japanese bronzes and porcelain. With this she declared Europe to be exhausted, and she frankly avowed that she was American to the tips of her fingers; she neither knew nor greatly cared whether America or Europe was best to live in; she had no violent love for either, and she had no objection to abusing both; but she meant to get all that American life had to offer, good or bad, and to drink it down to the dregs, fully determined that whatever there was in it she would have, and that whatever could be made out of it she would manufacture. "I know," said she, "that America produces petroleum and pigs; I have seen both on the steamers; and I am told it produces silver and gold. There is choice enough for any woman."

Yet, as has been already said, Mrs. Lee's first experience was not a success. She soon declared that New York might represent the petroleum or the pigs, but the gold of life was not to be discovered there by her eyes.

Recalling Facts

1. Mrs. Lee was born in
   - ☐ a. Philadelphia.
   - ☐ b. New York.
   - ☐ c. Boston.

2. Mrs. Lee's father was a
   - ☐ a. merchant.
   - ☐ b. clergyman.
   - ☐ c. writer.

3. Mrs. Lee traveled several times to
   - ☐ a. Canada.
   - ☐ b. Japan.
   - ☐ c. Europe.

4. Mrs. Lee decorated her home with
   - ☐ a. the works of American craftsmen.
   - ☐ b. foreign goods.
   - ☐ c. secondhand articles.

5. Mrs. Lee believed the gold of life was not to be found in
   - ☐ a. Europe.
   - ☐ b. New York.
   - ☐ c. Baltimore.

Understanding the Passage

6. Mrs. Lee appeared to be
   - ☐ a. somewhat unsatisfied.
   - ☐ b. enjoying life.
   - ☐ c. rude to strangers.

7. Mrs. Lee apparently had
   - ☐ a. no taste in furniture.
   - ☐ b. never considered relocating.
   - ☐ c. made a name for herself.

8. Mrs. Lee liked to
   - ☐ a. shop.
   - ☐ b. criticize.
   - ☐ c. both a and b.

9. When it came to the United States, Mrs. Lee felt
   - ☐ a. extreme loyalty.
   - ☐ b. no great passion.
   - ☐ c. heartsick.

10. Mrs. Lee can best be described as a person who
    - ☐ a. will never be totally satisfied.
    - ☐ b. would make a good friend.
    - ☐ c. spent money carefully.

from **Oliver Twist** *by Charles Dickens*

In great families, when an advantageous place cannot be obtained, either in possession, reversion, remainder, or expectancy, for the young man who is growing up, it is a very general custom to send him to sea. The workhouse board, in imitation of so wise and salutary an example, took counsel together on the expediency of shipping off Oliver Twist, in some small trading vessel bound to a good unhealthy port. This suggested itself as the very best thing that could possibly be done for him: the probability being, that the skipper would flog him to death, in a playful mood, someday ● after dinner, or would knock his brains out with an iron bar; both pastimes being, as it pretty generally known, very favorite and common recreations among gentlemen of that class. The more the case presented itself to the board, in this point of view, the more manifold the advantages of the step appeared; so, they came to the conclusion that the only way of providing for Oliver effectually, was to send him to sea without delay.

Mr. Bumble had been dispatched to make various preliminary inquiries, with the view of finding out some captain or other who wanted a cabin ● boy without any friends. He was returning to the workhouse to communicate the result of his mission when he encountered Mr. Sowerberry, the parochial undertaker.

Mr. Sowerberry was a tall, gaunt, large-jointed man, attired in a suit of threadbare black, with darned cotton stockings of the same color, and shoes to answer. His features were not naturally intended to wear a smiling aspect, but he was in general rather given to professional jocosity. His step was elastic, and his face betokened inward pleasantry, as he advanced to Mr. Bumble, and shook him cordially by the hand.

"I have taken the measure of the two women that died last night, Mr. ● Bumble," said the undertaker.

"You'll make your fortune, Mr. Sowerberry," said the beadle, as he thrust his thumb and forefinger into the proffered snuffbox of the undertaker: which was an ingenious little model of a patent coffin. "I say you'll make your fortune, Mr. Sowerberry," repeated Mr. Bumble, tapping the undertaker on the shoulder, in a friendly manner, with his cane.

"Think so?" said the undertaker in a tone which half admitted and half disputed the probability of the event. "The prices allowed by the board are very small, Mr. Bumble."

Recalling Facts

1. The common custom was to send a young boy without a future
   - ☐ a. to reform school.
   - ☐ b. to the sweatshops.
   - ☐ c. off to sea.

2. Mr. Bumble went out to look for
   - ☐ a. a captain.
   - ☐ b. an undertaker.
   - ☐ c. some friends.

3. Mr. Sowerberry dressed in
   - ☐ a. red.
   - ☐ b. green.
   - ☐ c. black.

4. The snuffbox was made in the shape of a
   - ☐ a. ship.
   - ☐ b. coffin.
   - ☐ c. tombstone.

5. Mr. Bumble thought Mr. Sowerberry would soon
   - ☐ a. make his fortune.
   - ☐ b. retire.
   - ☐ c. join the board.

Understanding the Passage

6. The board wanted to
   - ☐ a. quickly send Oliver Twist away.
   - ☐ b. help Oliver Twist.
   - ☐ c. please Mr. Sowerberry.

7. In those days a ship's captain was often
   - ☐ a. quite cruel.
   - ☐ b. stern but well-meaning.
   - ☐ c. generous with his crew.

8. Oliver's qualifications for being a cabin boy were
   - ☐ a. impressive.
   - ☐ b. minimal.
   - ☐ c. unknown to Mr. Bumble.

9. Mr. Bumble seemed to be promising Mr. Sowerberry
   - ☐ a. lots of work.
   - ☐ b. a box of snuff.
   - ☐ c. a new set of clothes.

10. Apparently people at the workhouse
    - ☐ a. lived full, rich lives.
    - ☐ b. were related to members of the board.
    - ☐ c. were treated poorly.

38   *from* The Life, Adventures & Piracies of the Famous Captain Singleton *by Daniel Defoe*

The island of Ceylon being inhabited for the greatest part by barbarians, which will not allow trade or commerce with any European nation, and inaccessible by any travelers, it will be convenient to relate the occasion how the author of this story happened to go into this island, and what opportunities he had of being fully acquainted with the people, their laws and customs, that so we may the better depend upon the account, and value it as it deserves, for the rarity as well as the truth of it; and of both these the author gives us a brief account. His words are as follows:

In the year 1657, the Anne frigate, of London, Captain Robert Knox, commander, on the 21st day of January, set sail out of the Downs, in the service of the honorable East India Company of England, bound for Fort St. George, upon the coast of Coromandel, to trade for one year from port to port in India; which having performed, as he was lading his goods to return for England, being in the road of Masulipatam, on the 19th of November 1659, there happened such a mighty storm, that in it several ships were cast away, and he was forced to cut his mainmast by the board, which so disabled the ship, that he could not proceed in his voyage; whereupon Cottiar, in the island of Ceylon, being a very commodious bay, fit for her present distress, Thomas Chambers, Esq., since Sir Thomas Chambers, the agent at Fort St. George, ordered that the ship should take in some cloth and India merchants belonging to Porto Novo, who might trade there while she lay to set her mast, and repair the other damages sustained by the storm. At her first coming thither, after the Indian merchants were set ashore, the captain and his men were very jealous of the people of that place, by reason the English never had any commerce or dealing with them; but after they had been there twenty days, going ashore and returning again at pleasure, without any molestation, they began to lay aside all suspicious thoughts of the people that dwelt thereabouts, who had kindly entertained them for their money.

By this time the king of the country had notice of their arrival, and, not being acquainted with their intents, he sent down a dissauva, or general, with an army.

Recalling Facts

1. The "barbarians" of Ceylon did not allow any trade
   □ a. with neighboring islands.
   □ b. with Europeans.
   □ c. among themselves.

2. This passage describes events which took place during the
   □ a. 15th century.
   □ b. 16th century.
   □ c. 17th century.

3. Fort St. George was located on the coast of
   □ a. Coromandel.
   □ b. England.
   □ c. Downs.

4. On November 19,
   □ a. a mighty storm hit.
   □ b. the *Anne* left England.
   □ c. Robert Knox took command of the *Anne*.

5. When the king became aware of the arrival of the English, he sent
   □ a. a general to investigate.
   □ b. warmest greetings.
   □ c. a death threat.

Understanding the Passage

6. At first, the ship's crew thought that the "barbarians" of Ceylon
   □ a. prospered from the trade industry.
   □ b. wanted to board the ship.
   □ c. hated white foreigners.

7. The original goal of the *Anne* was to trade with the
   □ a. Ceylonese.
   □ b. Indians.
   □ c. English.

8. The storm
   □ a. disabled the *Anne*.
   □ b. spared the *Anne*.
   □ c. briefly delayed the *Anne*

9. After a few weeks, the English slowly
   □ a. began to drop their prejudices.
   □ b. grew to hate the Indian traders.
   □ c. began to resent Thomas Chambers.

10. The king of the country
    □ a. knew all about the English.
    □ b. was suspicious of the intentions of the English.
    □ c. was afraid to confront the English.

Professor Lucifer had himself invented the flying machine, and had also invented nearly everything in it. All the tools of Professor Lucifer were the ancient human tools gone mad, grown into unrecognizable shapes, forgetful of their origin, forgetful of their names. That thing which looked like an enormous key with three wheels was really a very deadly revolver. That object which seemed to be created by the entanglement of two corkscrews was really the key. The thing which might have been mistaken for a tricycle turned upside down was the inexpressibly important instrument to which the corkscrew was the key. All these things the professor had invented; he had invented everything in the flying ship, with the exception, perhaps, of himself. This he had been born too late actually to inaugurate, but he believed, at least, that he had considerably improved it.

There was, however, another man on board, so to speak, at the time. Him, also, by a curious coincidence, the professor had not invented, and him he had not even very greatly improved, though he had fished him up with a lasso out of his own back garden, in Western Bulgaria, with the pure object of improving him. He was an exceedingly old man, almost entirely covered with white hair. You could see nothing but his eyes, and he seemed to talk with them. A monk of immense learning and acute intellect; he had made himself happy in a little stone hut and a little stone garden in the Balkans, chiefly by writing the crushing refutations and exposures of certain heresies, the last professors of which had been burnt (generally by each other) precisely 1,119 years previously. They were really very plausible and thoughtful heresies, and it was really a creditable or even glorious circumstance, that the old monk had been intellectual enough to detect their fallacy; the only misfortune was that nobody in the modern world was intellectual enough even to understand their argument. The old monk, one of whose names was Michael, and the other a name quite impossible to remember or repeat in our Western civilization, had, however, as I have said, made himself quite happy while he was in a mountain hermitage in the society of wild animals. And now that his luck had lifted him above all the mountains in the society of a wild physicist, he made himself happy still.

Recalling Facts

1. The tools of Professor Lucifer
   - ☐ a. were Michael's inventions.
   - ☐ b. began as ancient human tools.
   - ☐ c. were very sophisticated and expensive.

2. The thing that looked like an enormous key with three wheels was really
   - ☐ a. a deadly revolver.
   - ☐ b. an old corkscrew.
   - ☐ c. an upside down tricycle.

3. The other man on board the flying ship was a
   - ☐ a. doctor.
   - ☐ b. monk.
   - ☐ c. teacher.

4. The professor picked Michael up in order to
   - ☐ a. improve him.
   - ☐ b. learn from him.
   - ☐ c. discuss religion.

5. The professor was a
   - ☐ a. physician.
   - ☐ b. physicist.
   - ☐ c. philologist.

Understanding the Passage

6. Things aboard the flying ship could best be described as
   - ☐ a. simple and effective tools.
   - ☐ b. unusual concoctions.
   - ☐ c. worthless devices.

7. Apparently, the professor
   - ☐ a. loved to invent things.
   - ☐ b. was very lazy.
   - ☐ c. had many companions.

8. The professor captured Michael by
   - ☐ a. luring him with a new invention.
   - ☐ b. offering him a large sum of money.
   - ☐ c. roping him into the flying ship.

9. Michael appeared to be
   - ☐ a. too smart for the modern world.
   - ☐ b. a rather poor gardener.
   - ☐ c. miserable living in the Balkans.

10. Michael's reaction to being with the professor showed that he was
   - ☐ a. intolerant.
   - ☐ b. a heretic.
   - ☐ c. quite flexible.

from **The Story of an Heir** *by Joseph Addison*

Eudoxus and Leontine began the world with small estates. They were both of them men of good sense and great virtue; they prosecuted their studies together in their earlier years, and entered into such a friendship as lasted to the end of their lives. Eudoxus, at his first setting out in the world, threw himself into a court, where by his natural endowments and his acquired abilities, he raised a very considerable fortune. Leontine on the contrary sought all opportunities of improving his mind by study, conversation and travel; he was not only acquainted with all the sciences, but with the most eminent professors of them throughout Europe. He knew perfectly well the interests of its princes, with the customs and fashions of their courts, and could scarce meet with the name of an extraordinary person in the *Gazette* whom he had not either talked to or seen. In short, he had so well mixed and digested his knowledge of men and books, that he made one of the most accomplished persons of his age. During the whole course of his studies and travels he kept up a punctual correspondence with Eudoxus, who often made himself acceptable to the principal men about court by the intelligence which he received from Leontine. When they were both turned of forty they determined, pursuant to the resolution they had taken in the beginning of their lives, to retire, and pass the remainder of their days in the country. In order to do this, they both of them married much about the same time—Leontine, with his own and his wife's fortune, bought a farm of three hundred a year, which lay within the neighborhood of his friend Eudoxus, who had purchased an estate of as many thousands. They were both of them fathers about the same time, Eudoxus having a son born to him, and Leontine a daughter; but to the unspeakable grief of the latter, his young wife (in whom all his happiness was wrapped up) died in a few days after the birth of her daughter. His affliction would have been insupportable, had not he been comforted by the daily visits and con-versations of his friend. As they were one day talking together with their usual intimacy, Leontine, considering how incapable he was of giving his daughter a proper education in his own house, agreed with Eudoxus upon an exchange of children.

Recalling Facts

1. Eudoxus and Leontine were
   □ a. best friends.
   □ b. friends who became enemies.
   □ c. swindlers who made a fortune.

2. Leontine loved to
   □ a. make money.
   □ b. spend time at court.
   □ c. travel and study.

3. Both Eudoxus and Leontine married at the age of
   □ a. twenty.
   □ b. thirty.
   □ c. forty.

4. Leontine's young wife
   □ a. was unwilling to have more than one child.
   □ b. was penniless at the time of her marriage.
   □ c. died soon after the birth of her daughter.

5. Eudoxus and Leontine agreed to exchange
   □ a. wives.
   □ b. children.
   □ c. estates.

Understanding the Passage

6. Among professors of science Leontine was
   □ a. well known.
   □ b. largely unknown.
   □ c. scorned.

7. Leontine was well-read in areas of
   □ a. science.
   □ b. politics.
   □ c. many topics.

8. Leontine's letters helped Eudoxus to
   □ a. impress people at court.
   □ b. invest his money wisely
   □ c. find a wife.

9. The lives of Eudoxus and Leontine appeared to be
   □ a. well planned.
   □ b. disappointing to both men.
   □ c. chaotic.

10. Eudoxus's estate was apparently
   □ a. smaller than Leontine's.
   □ b. larger than Leontine's.
   □ c. about the same size as Leontine's.

While Giovanni Guasconti stood at the window, he heard a rustling behind a screen of leaves, and became aware that a person was at work in the garden. His figure soon emerged into view, and showed itself to be that of no common laborer, but a tall, emaciated, sallow, and sickly looking man, dressed in a scholar's garb of black. He was beyond the middle term of life, with gray hair, a thin gray beard, and a face singularly marked with intellect and cultivation, but which could never, even in his more youthful days, have expressed much warmth of heart.

Nothing could exceed the intentness with which this scientific gardener examined every shrub which grew in his path; it seemed as if he was looking into their inmost nature, making observations in regard to their creative essence, and discovering why one leaf grew in this shape, and another in that, and wherefore such and such flowers differed among themselves in hue and perfume. Nevertheless, in spite of the deep intelligence on his part, there was no approach to intimacy between himself and these vegetable existences. On the contrary, he avoided their actual touch, or the direct inhaling of their odors, with a caution that impressed Giovanni Guasconti most disagreeably; for the man's demeanor was that of one walking among malignant influences, such as savage beasts, or deadly snakes, or evil spirits, which, should he allow them one moment of license, would wreck upon him some terrible fatality. It was strangely frightful to the young man's imagination, to see this air of insecurity in a person cultivating a garden, that most simple and innocent of human toils, and which had been alike the joy and labor of the unfallen parents of the race. Was this garden, then the Eden of the present world?—and this man, with such a perception of harm in what his own hands caused to grow, was he the Adam?

The distrustful gardener, while plucking away the dead leaves or pruning the too luxuriant growth of the shrubs, defended his hands with a pair of thick gloves. Nor were these his only armor. When, in his walk through the garden, he came to the magnificent plant that hung its purple gems beside the marble fountain, he placed a kind of mask over his mouth and nostrils, as if all this beauty did but conceal a deadlier malice.

Recalling Facts

1. The old man in the garden was
   - ☐ a. sickly looking.
   - ☐ b. short and heavyset.
   - ☐ c. both a and b.

2. The face of the old man lacked
   - ☐ a. intelligence.
   - ☐ b. warmth.
   - ☐ c. cultivation.

3. Giovanni was disagreeably impressed by the old man's
   - ☐ a. carelessness.
   - ☐ b. caution.
   - ☐ c. slovenly clothing.

4. The narrator felt that the most simple and innocent of human toils was
   - ☐ a. observing the behavior of another person.
   - ☐ b. reading a book.
   - ☐ c. cultivating a garden.

5. The old man wore
   - ☐ a. heavy boots.
   - ☐ b. a long cloak.
   - ☐ c. thick gloves.

Understanding the Passage

6. The gardener appeared to be
   - ☐ a. having a pleasant time.
   - ☐ b. extremely serious.
   - ☐ c. unfamiliar with most plants.

7. The gardener acted as though he was walking through
   - ☐ a. the garden of a fabulous palace.
   - ☐ b. a place that held fond memories.
   - ☐ c. a place of displeasure and disease.

8. The behavior of the gardener
   - ☐ a. intrigued the narrator.
   - ☐ b. bored the narrator.
   - ☐ c. repelled the narrator.

9. Giovanni's style of gardening would probably have been
   - ☐ a. different from that of the old man's.
   - ☐ b. even more cautious than the old man's.
   - ☐ c. the same as the old man's.

10. The old man's personality could best be described as
    - ☐ a. lively and engaging.
    - ☐ b. sober and distant.
    - ☐ c. harsh and unforgiving.

In surgery, having the least experience, and it being a business that spoke directly to the senses, Elnathan Todd was most apt to distrust his own powers; but he had applied oils to several burns, cut round the roots of sundry defective teeth, and sewed up the wounds of numberless wood choppers, with considerable eclat, when an unfortunate jobber suffered a fracture of his leg by the tree that he had been felling. It was on this occasion that our hero encountered the greatest trial his nerves and moral feeling had ever sustained. In the hour of need, however, he was not found wanting. Most of the amputations in the new settlements, and they were quite frequent, were performed by one practitioner, who possessing originally a reputation, was enabled by this circumstance to acquire an experience that rendered him deserving of it, and Elnathan had been present at one or two of these operations. But on the present occasion the man of practice was not to be obtained, and the duty fell, as a matter of course, to the share of Mr. Todd. He went to work with a kind of blind desperation, observing, at the same time, the externals of decent gravity and great skill. The sufferer's name was Milligan, and it was to this event that Richard alluded when he spoke of assisting the Doctor at an amputation—by holding the leg! The limb was certainly cut off, and the patient survived the operation. It was, however, two years before poor Milligan ceased to complain that they had buried the leg in so narrow a box, that it was straitened for room; he could feel the pain shooting up from the inhumed fragment into the living members. Marmaduke suggested that the fault might lie in the arteries and nerves; but Richard, considering the amputation as part of his own handiwork, strongly repelled the insinuation, at the same time declaring that he had often heard of men who could tell when it was going to rain by the toes of amputated limbs. After two or three years, notwithstanding Milligan's complaints gradually diminished, the leg was dug up, and a larger box furnished, and from that hour no one heard the sufferer utter another complaint on the subject. This gave the public great confidence in Dr. Todd, whose reputation was hourly increasing, and, luckily for his patients, his information also.

Recalling Facts

1. Elnathan Todd earned his living by
   - ☐ a. chopping wood.
   - ☐ b. fixing wounds.
   - ☐ c. filling teeth.

2. The jobber had his leg fractured
   - ☐ a. climbing over a fence.
   - ☐ b. by a tree.
   - ☐ c. by a misdirected bullet.

3. In the moment of crisis, Elnathan Todd
   - ☐ a. panicked.
   - ☐ b. performed admirably.
   - ☐ c. let someone else operate.

4. Richard
   - ☐ a. broke his leg.
   - ☐ b. questioned Elnathan's ability.
   - ☐ c. assisted Elnathan.

5. Eventually, the amputated leg was
   - ☐ a. put in a larger box.
   - ☐ b. blamed for frequent heavy rains.
   - ☐ c. studied for medical purposes.

Understanding the Passage

6. Apparently, Elnathan Todd was not
   - ☐ a. well trained.
   - ☐ b. compassionate.
   - ☐ c. particularly courageous.

7. Work in the new settlement seems to have been
   - ☐ a. hazardous.
   - ☐ b. lucrative.
   - ☐ c. hard to find.

8. The regular practitioner
   - ☐ a. knew what he was doing from the start.
   - ☐ b. learned by trial and error.
   - ☐ c. knowingly gave Elnathan his big chance.

9. Richard was
   - ☐ a. proud of the job he and Elnathan had done.
   - ☐ b. embarrassed to admit he knew Milligan.
   - ☐ c. a better surgeon than Elnathan.

10. Apparently Milligan was not the first amputee to
    - ☐ a. have Elnathan Todd as his surgeon.
    - ☐ b. have the sensation of feeling in his severed limb
    - ☐ c. lose a huge amount of blood during the operation.

It was now debated whether Mr. Allworthy should be informed of the death of his sister. This the doctor violently opposed, but Mr. Blifil said he had received such positive and repeated orders from his uncle never to keep any secret from him for fear of the disquietude which it might give him, that he dare not think of disobedience, whatever might be the consequence. He said, for his part, considering the religious and philosophic temper of his uncle, he could not agree with the doctor in his aprehensions. He was therefore resolved to communicate it to him, for if his uncle recovered (as he heartily prayed he might) he knew he would never forgive an endeavor to keep a secret of this kind from him.

The physician was forced to submit to these resolutions. So together moved Mr. Blifil and the doctor toward the sickroom; where the physician first entered, and approached the bed, in order to feel his patient's pulse, which he had no sooner done that he declared he was much better; that the last application had succeeded to a miracle, and had brought the fever to intermit; so that, he said, there appeared now to be as little danger as he had before apprehended there were hopes.

To say the truth, Mr. Allworthy's situation had never been so bad as the great caution of the doctor had represented it; but as a wise general never despises his enemy, however inferior that enemy's force may be, so neither doth a wise physician ever despise a distemper, however inconsiderable. As the former preserves the same strict discipline, places the same guards, and employs the same scouts, though the enemy be never so weak, so the latter maintains the same gravity of countenance, and shakes his head with the same significant air, let the distemper be never so trifling. And both, among many other good ones, may assign this solid reason for their conduct, that by these means the greater glory redounds to them if they gain the victory, and the less disgrace if by any unlucky accident they should happen to be conquered.

Mr. Allworthy had no sooner lifted up his eyes, and thanked Heaven for these hopes of his recovery, than Mr. Blifil drew near, with a very dejected aspect, and communicated to his uncle what the reader hath been just before acquainted with.

Recalling Facts

1. The doctor did not want to
   tell Mr. Allworthy
   □ a. how serious his illness was.
   □ b. that Mr. Blifil was lying
       to him.
   □ c. about the death of his sister.

2. Mr. Blifil was Mr. Allworthy's
   □ a. uncle.
   □ b. brother.
   □ c. nephew.

3. As soon as the doctor entered
   the sickroom, he
   □ a. felt Mr. Allworthy's pulse.
   □ b. broke the bad news to
       Mr. Allworthy.
   □ c. gave Mr. Allworthy his
       medicine.

4. The narrator compared the
   doctor's attitude to that of a
   □ a. good attorney.
   □ b. wise general.
   □ c. courageous scout.

5. The bad news was
   □ a. withheld from Mr. Allworthy.
   □ b. announced by the doctor.
   □ c. announced by Mr. Blifil.

Understanding the Passage

6. The doctor and Mr. Blifil
   seemed to
   □ a. agree on all matters of
       Mr. Allworthy's care.
   □ b. argue over Mr.
       Allworthy's treatment.
   □ c. disagree on one
       major point.

7. Mr. Allworthy did not want
   □ a. his family to worry.
   □ b. to believe his doctor.
   □ c. bad news to be hidden
       from him.

8. Initially, the doctor
   □ a. made Mr. Allworthy's
       illness sound worse
       than it was.
   □ b. was extremely reticent
       to touch Mr. Allworthy.
   □ c. wanted Mr. Blifil to help
       him treat the patient.

9. The final decision about
   what to tell Mr. Allworthy
   rested with
   □ a. the doctor.
   □ b. Mr. Blifil.
   □ c. both men equally.

10. The doctor felt his treatment
    □ a. worked wonders.
    □ b. had no discernible
        impact.
    □ c. was controversial in
        medical circles.

44 *from* The Fall of the House of Usher *by Edgar Allan Poe*

During the whole of a dull, dark, and soundless day in the autumn of the year, when the clouds hung oppressively low in the heavens, I had been passing alone, on horseback, through a singularly dreary tract of country, and at length found myself, as the shades of the evening drew on, within view of the melancholy House of Usher. I know not how it was—but, with the first glimpse of the building, a sense of insufferable gloom pervaded my spirit. I say insufferable; for the feeling was unrelieved by any of that half-pleasurable, because poetic, sentiment with which the mind usually receives even the sternest natural images of the desolate or terrible. I looked upon the scene before me—upon the mere house, and the simple landscape features of the domain—upon the bleak walls—upon the vacant eyelike windows—upon a few rank sedges—and upon a few white trunks of decayed trees—with an utter depression of soul which I can compare to no earthly sensation more properly than to the afterdream of the reveler upon opium—the bitter lapse into everyday life—the hideous dropping off of the veil. There was an iciness, a sinking, a sickening of the heart—an unredeemed dreariness of thought which no goading of the imagination could torture into aught of the sublime. What was it—I paused to think—what was it that so unnerved me in the contemplation of the House of Usher? It was a mystery all insoluble; nor could I grapple with the shadowy fancies that crowded upon me as I pondered. I was forced to fall back upon the unsatisfactory conclusion, that while, beyond doubt, there *are* combinations of very simple natural objects which have the power of thus affecting us, still the analysis of this power lies among considerations beyond our depth. It was possible, I reflected, that a mere different arrangement of the particulars of the scene, of the details of the picture, would be sufficient to modify, or perhaps to annihilate its capacity for sorrowful impression; and, acting upon this idea, I reined my horse to the precipitous brink of a black and lurid pool that lay in unruffled luster by the dwelling, and gazed down—but with a shudder even more thrilling than before—upon the remodeled and inverted images of the gray sedge, and the ghastly tree stems, and the vacant and eyelike windows.

Recalling Facts

1. The narrator was traveling
   - ☐ a. on foot.
   - ☐ b. by carriage.
   - ☐ c. on horseback.

2. When the House of Usher came into the narrator's view, it was
   - ☐ a. dawn.
   - ☐ b. early evening.
   - ☐ c. midnight.

3. The narrator describes the windows as
   - ☐ a. vacant.
   - ☐ b. eyelike.
   - ☐ c. both a and b.

4. The narrator found the sight of the House of Usher to be
   - ☐ a. unnerving.
   - ☐ b. ordinary.
   - ☐ c. delightful.

5. At the brink the narrator gazed down on a
   - ☐ a. barn.
   - ☐ b. pool.
   - ☐ c. village.

Understanding the Passage

6. After seeing the House of Usher, the narrator felt
   - ☐ a. depressed.
   - ☐ b. inspired.
   - ☐ c. relaxed.

7. Images of the desolate
   - ☐ a. always terrify.
   - ☐ b. are found only in the country.
   - ☐ c. can usually be modified.

8. Hoping to lessen his sense of depression, the narrator
   - ☐ a. entered the house.
   - ☐ b. stopped his horse.
   - ☐ c. quickly withdrew.

9. The reason the House of Usher was so terrifying
   - ☐ a. remained unknown to the narrator.
   - ☐ b. was known to everyone.
   - ☐ c. could be easily explained.

10. The narrator's efforts to shake off his depression
    - ☐ a. were successful.
    - ☐ b. made him physically ill.
    - ☐ c. were purely intellectual

The more I dive into this matter of whaling, so much the more am I impressed with its great honorableness and antiquity; and especially when I find so many great demigods and heroes, prophets of all sorts, who one way or other have shed distinction upon it, I am transported with the reflection that I myself belong, though but subordinately, to so emblazoned a fraternity.

The gallant Perseus, a son of Jupiter, was the first whaleman; and to the eternal honor of our calling be it said, that the first whale attacked by our brotherhood was not killed with any sordid intent. Those were the knightly days of our profession, when we only bore arms to succor the distressed, and not to fill men's lamp feeders. Everyone knows the fine story of Perseus and Andromeda; how the lovely Andromeda, the daughter of a king, was tied to a rock on the seacoast, and as Leviathan was in the very act of carrying her off, Perseus, the prince of whalemen, intrepidly advancing, harpooned the monster, and delivered and married the maid. It was an admirable artistic exploit, rarely achieved by harpooneers of the present day; inasmuch as this Leviathan was slain at the very first dart. And let no man doubt this story; for in the ancient Joppa, on the Syrian coast, in one of the pagan temples, there stood for many ages the vast skeleton of a whale, which the city's legends and all the inhabitants asserted to be the identical bones of the monster that Perseus slew. When the Romans took Joppa, the same skeleton was carried to Italy in triumph. What seems most singular and suggestively important in this story, is this: it was from Joppa that Jonah set sail.

Akin to this adventure of Perseus and Andromeda—indeed, by some supposed to be indirectly derived from it—is that famous story of St. George and the Dragon; which dragon I maintain to have been a whale; for in many old chronicles whales and dragons are strangely jumbled together, and often stand for each other. "Thou art as a lion of the waters, and as a dragon of sea," saith Ezekiel; hereby, plainly meaning a whale. Besides, it would much subtract from the glory of the exploit had St. George but encountered a crawling reptile of the land, instead of doing battle with the great monster of the deep.

Recalling Facts

1. What really impressed the narrator about whaling was its
   - ☐ a. savage and bloody encounters.
   - ☐ b. many heroes.
   - ☐ c. profitable nature.

2. The first whaleman was Jupiter's son,
   - ☐ a. Perseus.
   - ☐ b. Andromeda.
   - ☐ c. Leviathan.

3. Andromeda was tied to a
   - ☐ a. bow.
   - ☐ b. pier.
   - ☐ c. rock.

4. The bones of the first slain whale could be found in
   - ☐ a. a pagan temple.
   - ☐ b. an Egyptian pyramid.
   - ☐ c. a Roman mausoleum.

5. In many old stories, whales were often confused with
   - ☐ a. dinosaurs.
   - ☐ b. dragons.
   - ☐ c. sea serpents.

Understanding the Passage

6. The narrator felt that he had
   - ☐ a. joined a select group.
   - ☐ b. misunderstood the history of whaling.
   - ☐ c. written a complete account of whaling.

7. The first whale was killed
   - ☐ a. for its oil.
   - ☐ b. for food.
   - ☐ c. in a rescue mission.

8. "The Leviathan" referred to
   - ☐ a. Perseus.
   - ☐ b. a whale.
   - ☐ c. a giant dragon.

9. The Romans apparently prized
   - ☐ a. pagan temples.
   - ☐ b. the skeleton of the whale.
   - ☐ c. freedom for the citizens of Joppa.

10. The narrator implied that most modern harpooneers could not
    - ☐ a. locate whales with any reliability.
    - ☐ b. kill a whale with a single harpoon.
    - ☐ c. understand the true nature of whales.

Paley, a common authority with many on moral questions, in his chapter on the "Duty of Submission to Civil Government," resolves all civil obligation into expediency; and he proceeds to say, "that so long as the interest of the whole society requires it, that is, so long as the established government cannot be resisted or changed without public inconveniency, it is the will of God that the established government be obeyed, and no longer. . . . This principle being admitted, the justice of every particular case of resistance is reduced to a computation of the quantity of the danger and grievance on the one side, and of the probability and expense of redressing it on the other." But Paley appears never to have contemplated those cases to which the rule of expediency does not apply, in which a people, as well as an individual, must do justice, cost what it may. If I have unjustly wrested a plank from a drowning man, I must restore it to him though I drown myself. This, according to Paley, would be inconvenient; but he that would save his life, in such a case, shall lose it. This people must cease to hold slaves, and to make war on Mexico, though it cost them their existence as a people.

In their practice, nations agree with Paley; but does anyone think that Massachusetts does exactly what is right at the present crisis?

Practically speaking, the opponents to a reform in Massachusetts are not a hundred thousand politicians at the South, but a hundred thousand merchants and farmers here, who are more interested in commerce and agriculture than they are in humanity, and are not prepared to do justice to the slave and to Mexico, *cost what it may*. I quarrel not with far-off foes, but with those who, near at home, cooperate with, and do the bidding of, those far away, and without whom the latter would be harmless. We are accustomed to say that the mass of men are unprepared; but improvement is slow, because the few are not materially wiser or better than the many. It is not so important that many should be as good as you, as that there be some absolute goodness somewhere; for that will leaven the whole lump. There are thousands who are *in opinion* opposed to slavery and to the war, who yet in effect do nothing.

Recalling Facts

1. Paley based all civil obligation on
   - ☐ a. friendship.
   - ☐ b. loyalty.
   - ☐ c. expediency.

2. The narrator believed that there were times when
   - ☐ a. people must do the right thing regardless of the cost.
   - ☐ b. slavery could be justified.
   - ☐ c. both a and b.

3. The narrator wanted the United States to stop
   - ☐ a. the war on Mexico.
   - ☐ b. the publication of Paley's books.
   - ☐ c. believing in the will of God.

4. According to the narrator, the real opponents of reform were the
   - ☐ a. politicians of the South.
   - ☐ b. farmers and merchants of Massachusetts.
   - ☐ c. slaveholders in Mexico.

5. The narrator believed in the necessity of
   - ☐ a. regular elections.
   - ☐ b. absolute goodness.
   - ☐ c. reading Paley.

Understanding the Passage

6. Paley believed in
   - ☐ a. the will of God.
   - ☐ b. justice based on individual consciousness.
   - ☐ c. civil disobedience.

7. Paley viewed justice as a
   - ☐ a. mathematical equation.
   - ☐ b. personal judgment.
   - ☐ c. notion based on absolute goodness.

8. To the narrator, slavery and the war with Mexico were
   - ☐ a. political issues.
   - ☐ b. economic issues.
   - ☐ c. moral issues.

9. The narrator believed that reform must
   - ☐ a. begin in Congress.
   - ☐ b. start with the individual.
   - ☐ c. address foreign enemies first.

10. According to the narrator, the individual's role in reform is
    - ☐ a. insignificant.
    - ☐ b. of some limited value.
    - ☐ c. very important.

In the first place, Cranford is in possession of the Amazons; all the holders of houses above a certain rent are women. If a married couple come to settle in the town, somehow the gentleman disappears; he is either fairly frightened to death by being the only man in the Cranford evening parties, or he is accounted for by being with his regiment, his ship, or closely engaged in business all the week in the great neighboring commercial town of Drumble, distant only twenty miles on a railroad. In short, whatever does become of the gentlemen, they are not at Cranford. What could they do if they were there? The surgeon has his round of thirty miles, sleeps at Cranford, but every man cannot be a surgeon. For keeping the trim gardens full of choice flowers without a weed to speck them; for frightening away little boys who look wistfully at the said flowers through the railings; for the rushing out at the geese that occasionally venture into the gardens if the gates are left open; for deciding all the questions of literature and politics without troubling themselves with unnecessary reasons or arguments; for obtaining clear and correct knowledge of everybody's affairs in the parish; for keeping their neat maidservants in admirable order; for kindness (somewhat dictatorial) to the poor, and real tender good offices to each other whenever they are in distress, the ladies of Cranford are quite sufficient. "A man," as one of them observed to me once, "is *so* in the way in the house." Although the ladies of Cranford know all each other's proceedings, they are exceedingly indifferent to each other's opinions. Indeed, as each has her own individuality, not to say eccentricity, pretty strongly developed, nothing is so easy as verbal retaliation, but, somehow, goodwill reigns among them to a considerable degree.

The Cranford ladies have only an occasional little quarrel, spurted out in a few peppery words and angry jerks of the head, just enough to prevent the even tenor of their lives from becoming too flat. Their dress is very independent of fashion; as they observe, "What does it signify how we dress here at Cranford, where everybody knows us?" And if they go from home, their reason is equally cogent, "What does it signify how we dress here, where nobody knows us?" The materials of their clothes are, in general, good and plain.

Recalling Facts

1. Cranford was notable for its lack of
   - ☐ a. women.
   - ☐ b. gentlemen.
   - ☐ c. flowers.

2. Drumble was a
   - ☐ a. town.
   - ☐ b. surgeon.
   - ☐ c. gardener.

3. The ladies of Cranford did not care about each other's
   - ☐ a. goodwill.
   - ☐ b. children.
   - ☐ c. opinions.

4. The ladies of Cranford were not
   - ☐ a. strong willed.
   - ☐ b. slaves to fashion.
   - ☐ c. the type ever to quarrel.

5. Clothing materials in Cranford were
   - ☐ a. fine and expensive.
   - ☐ b. generally of poor quality.
   - ☐ c. good but plain.

Understanding the Passage

6. The women in Cranford can best be described as
   - ☐ a. self-sufficient.
   - ☐ b. typical housewives.
   - ☐ c. cold and ambitious.

7. A gentleman in Cranford would
   - ☐ a. enjoy the company of so many women.
   - ☐ b. soon leave town.
   - ☐ c. want to run the town's business.

8. The surgeon
   - ☐ a. avoided Cranford.
   - ☐ b. visited Cranford regularly.
   - ☐ c. wasn't allowed to practice medicine in Cranford.

9. The ladies of Cranford found men to be
   - ☐ a. a general nuisance.
   - ☐ b. useful around the house
   - ☐ c. fun to argue with.

10. The ladies of Cranford did not care what other people thought of their
    - ☐ a. physical appearance.
    - ☐ b. taste in literature and politics.
    - ☐ c. both a and b.

Whoever has made a voyage up the Hudson must remember the Catskill Mountains. They are a dismembered branch of the great Appalachian family, and are seen away to the west of the river swelling up to noble height. Every change of season, every change of weather, indeed every hour of the day, produces some change in the magical hues and shapes of these mountains, and they are regarded by all the good wives far and near as perfect barometers.

At the foot of these fairy mountains the voyager may have descried the light smoke curling up from a village, whose shingle roofs gleam among the trees, just where the blue tints of the upland melt away into the fresh green of the nearer landscape. It is a little village of great antiquity, having been founded by some of the Dutch colonists in the early times of the province, just about the beginning of the government of the good Peter Stuyvesant, and there were some of the houses of the original settlers standing within a few years, built of small yellow bricks brought from Holland, having latticed windows and gable fronts, surmounted with weathercocks.

In that same village, and in one of these very houses (which to tell the precise truth was sadly timeworn and weather-beaten) there lived many years since, while the country was yet a province of Great Britain, a simple good-natured fellow of the name of Rip Van Winkle. He was a descendant of the Van Winkles who figured so gallantly in the chivalrous days of Peter Stuyvesant, and accompanied him to the siege of Fort Christina. He inherited, however, but little of the martial character of his ancestors. I have observed that he was a simple good-natured man; he was moreover a kind neighbor, and an obedient, henpecked husband. Indeed to the latter circumstance might be owing that meekness of spirit which gained him such universal popularity; for those men are most apt to be obsequious and conciliating abroad, who are under the discipline of shrews at home. Their tempers doubtless are rendered pliant and malleable in the fiery furnace of domestic tribulation, and a curtain lecture is worth all the sermons in the world for teaching the virtues of patience and long suffering. A termagant wife may therefore in some respects be considered a tolerable blessing—and if so, Rip Van Winkle was thrice blessed.

Recalling Facts

1. The Catskills are described as a dismembered branch of the
   - a. Rocky Mountains.
   - b. Appalachian Mountains.
   - c. Green Mountains.

2. The Catskill Mountains change hue
   - a. never.
   - b. rarely.
   - c. frequently.

3. The village described in the passage was founded by
   - a. the Van Winkles.
   - b. Dutch colonists.
   - c. the Stuyvesant family.

4. The houses of the original settlers were made of
   - a. pine and maple logs.
   - b. small yellow bricks.
   - c. stone and mud.

5. Rip Van Winkle was a
   - a. stingy man.
   - b. brilliant scholar.
   - c. kind neighbor.

Understanding the Passage

6. The early settlers in the village
   - a. had never heard of Peter Stuyvesant.
   - b. did not recognize the authority of Great Britain
   - c. were familiar with the Van Winkle family.

7. Apparently Rip Van Winkle's wife was a
   - a. demanding woman.
   - b. sickly woman.
   - c. compassionate woman.

8. The narrator feels that henpecked husbands
   - a. often die at an early age.
   - b. are often very popular in the community.
   - c. know little about marital arts.

9. Rip Van Winkle could best be described as
   - a. thoughtless.
   - b. mild mannered.
   - c. bitter.

10. Rip Van Winkle's ancestors were apparently
    - a. famous craftsmen.
    - b. a downtrodden lot.
    - c. brave warriors.

In the days when spinning wheels hummed busily in farmhouses, there might be seen deep in the bosom of the hills, certain pallid undersized men, who, by the side of the brawny country folk, looked like the remnants of a disinherited race. The shepherd's dog barked fiercely when one of these alien-looking men appeared on the upland, dark against the early winter sunset; for what dog likes a figure bent under a heavy bag?—and these pale men rarely stirred abroad without that mysterious burden. The shepherd himself, though he had good reason to believe that the bag held nothing but flaxen thread, or else long rolls of strong linen spun from that thread, was not quite sure that this trade of weaving, indispensable though it was, could be carried on entirely without the help of the Evil One. In that far-off time superstition clung easily round every person or thing that was at all unwonted, or even intermittent and occasional. No one knew where wandering men had their homes or their origin; and how was a man to be explained unless you at least knew somebody who knew his father and mother? To the peasants of old times, the world outside their own direct experience was a region of vagueness and mystery: to their untraveled thought a state of wandering was a conception as dim as the winter life of the swallows that came back with the spring; and even a settler, if he came from distant parts, hardly ever ceased to be viewed with a remnant of distrust, which would have prevented any surprise if a long course of inoffensive conduct on his part had ended in the commission of a crime, especially if he had any reputation for knowledge, or showed any skill in handicraft. All cleverness, whether in the rapid use of that difficult instrument the tongue, or in some other art unfamiliar to villagers, was in itself suspicious: honest folk, born and bred in a visible manner, were mostly not overwise or clever—at least, not beyond such a matter as knowing the signs of the weather; and the process by which rapidity and dexterity of any kind were acquired was so wholly hidden, that they partook of the nature of conjuring. In this way it came to pass that those scattered linen weavers—emigrants from town into country—were to the last regarded as aliens by their rustic neighbors.

Recalling Facts

1. When a shepherd dog saw an alien-looking man, it would
   - ☐ a. turn and run away.
   - ☐ b. bark fiercely.
   - ☐ c. whimper and edge closer to its master.

2. Weavers carried with them
   - ☐ a. heavy bags of thread and linen.
   - ☐ b. spinning wheels.
   - ☐ c. remnants of their ancestors' clothing.

3. Honest country folk were not
   - ☐ a. overly wise.
   - ☐ b. brawny.
   - ☐ c. suspicious of strangers.

4. Linen weavers were emigrants from
   - ☐ a. town to city.
   - ☐ b. country to city.
   - ☐ c. town to country.

5. The narrator felt that most peasants were only clever enough to
   - ☐ a. recognize the signs of the weather.
   - ☐ b. spin flaxen thread into linen.
   - ☐ c. display a dexterity with language.

Understanding the Passage

6. Compared to most country folk, weavers were not
   - ☐ a. physically strong.
   - ☐ b. well educated.
   - ☐ c. polite.

7. Peasants trusted only
   - ☐ a. their relatives.
   - ☐ b. people with known family.
   - ☐ c. deeply religious men.

8. Peasants tended to equate nimble hands with
   - ☐ a. intelligence.
   - ☐ b. dim minds.
   - ☐ c. evil spirits.

9. Peasants were not surprised when outsiders
   - ☐ a. married local youths.
   - ☐ b. committed crimes.
   - ☐ c. lived quiet lives.

10. Most weavers were never
    - ☐ a. fully accepted into country society.
    - ☐ b. strong enough to carry a full bag of linen.
    - ☐ c. found far from their ancestral home.

The year 1747 is distinguished as the epoch, when Samuel Johnson's arduous and important work, his *Dictionary of the English Language*, was announced to the world, by the publication of its Plan or Prospectus.

How long this immense undertaking had been the object of his contemplation, I do not know. I once asked him by what means he had attained to that astonishing knowledge of our language, by which he was enabled to realize a design of such extent and accumulated difficulty. He told me that it was not the effect of particular study, but that it had grown up in his mind insensibly. I have been informed by Mr. James Dodsley, that several years before this period, when Johnson was one day sitting in his brother Robert's shop, he heard his brother suggest to him that a dictionary of the English language would be a work that would be well received by the public; that Johnson seemed at first to catch at the proposition, but, after a pause, said, in his abrupt decisive manner, "I believe I shall not undertake it."

The booksellers who contracted with Johnson for the execution of a work, which in other countries has not been effected but by the cooperating exertions of many, were Mr. Robert Dodsley, Mr. Charles Hitch, Mr. Andrew Millar, the two Messieurs Longman, and the two Messieurs Knapton. The price stipulated was fifteen hundred and seventy-five pounds.

The Plan was addressed to Philip Dormer, Earl of Chesterfield, then one of his Majesty's Principal Secretaries of State, a nobleman who was very ambitious of literary distinction and who, upon being informed of the design, had expressed himself in terms very favorable to its success. There is, perhaps, in everything of any consequence, a secret history which it would be amusing to know, could we have it authentically communicated. Johnson told me, "Sir, the way in which the plan of my dictionary came to be inscribed to Lord Chesterfield, was this: I had neglected to write it by the time appointed. Dodsley suggested it be addressed to Lord Chesterfield. I laid hold of this as a pretext for delay, that it might be better done, and let Dodsley have his desire. I said to my friend, Dr. Bathurst, 'Now if any good comes of my addressing to Lord Chesterfield, it will be ascribed to deep policy,' when it was only a casual excuse for laziness."

Recalling Facts

1. The narrator did now know how long Johnson had been
   - ☐ a. working with co-editors.
   - ☐ b. lecturing at the university.
   - ☐ c. planning to write a dictionary.

2. The narrator looked upon Johnson's project as
   - ☐ a. extremely difficult.
   - ☐ b. relatively straightforward.
   - ☐ c. fit only for fools.

3. Johnson's brother Robert had once suggested that Johnson
   - ☐ a. become a bookseller.
   - ☐ b. write a dictionary.
   - ☐ c. meet with Philip Dormer.

4. Philip Dormer was
   - ☐ a. a bookseller.
   - ☐ b. the Earl of Chesterfield.
   - ☐ c. Johnson's partner.

5. Dr. Bathurst was a friend of
   - ☐ a. Samuel Johnson.
   - ☐ b. Lord Chesterfield.
   - ☐ c. Mr. Robert Dodsley.

Understanding the Passage

6. Johnson's book was
   - ☐ a. generally ignored.
   - ☐ b. of interest only to scholars.
   - ☐ c. a monumental achievement.

7. Johnson's decision to do this project came
   - ☐ a. quickly and impulsively
   - ☐ b. after he was offered sufficient payment.
   - ☐ c. over a long period of time.

8. At first Johnson thought that such a project was
   - ☐ a. utterly impossible.
   - ☐ b. tempting, but not for him.
   - ☐ c. beneath his dignity.

9. The booksellers mentioned in the passage seemed to regard the project with
   - ☐ a. enthusiasm.
   - ☐ b. suspicion.
   - ☐ c. amusement.

10. Johnson looked upon Dodsley's suggestion as
   - ☐ a. an excuse to get more time.
   - ☐ b. the talk of a bitter man.
   - ☐ c. inappropriate at the time.

Answer Key

Progress Graph

Pacing Graph

Answer Key

1 1. c 2. c 3. b 4. a 5. c 6. c 7. b 8. a 9. c 10. c

2 1. b 2. b 3. a 4. c 5. a 6. c 7. b 8. b 9. a 10. c

3 1. a 2. c 3. c 4. a 5. c 6. b 7. a 8. c 9. c 10. c

4 1. b 2. b 3. b 4. c 5. a 6. c 7. a 8. a 9. c 10. a

5 1. a 2. b 3. b 4. b 5. a 6. c 7. b 8. c 9. a 10. b

6 1. c 2. b 3. a 4. a 5. a 6. b 7. a 8. a 9. b 10. b

7 1. c 2. b 3. c 4. a 5. b 6. b 7. c 8. c 9. a 10. c

8 1. a 2. a 3. c 4. b 5. c 6. a 7. a 8. c 9. a 10. b

9 1. b 2. c 3. b 4. a 5. b 6. a 7. a 8. b 9. a 10. b

10 1. c 2. c 3. b 4. c 5. b 6. c 7. a 8. a 9. b 10. a

11 1. c 2. b 3. c 4. c 5. c 6. b 7. b 8. b 9. c 10. a

12 1. b 2. c 3. a 4. b 5. b 6. a 7. a 8. c 9. a 10. b

13 1. a 2. c 3. b 4. a 5. b 6. c 7. b 8. a 9. b 10. b

14 1. c 2. c 3. b 4. b 5. b 6. a 7. c 8. a 9. c 10. b

15 1. a 2. c 3. a 4. b 5. a 6. c 7. b 8. c 9. a 10. a

16 1. a 2. b 3. c 4. c 5. a 6. a 7. b 8. c 9. c 10. c

17 1. c 2. a 3. b 4. b 5. a 6. a 7. c 8. a 9. c 10. a

18 1. c 2. a 3. b 4. a 5. c 6. c 7. b 8. b 9. b 10. b

19 1. b 2. a 3. a 4. c 5. c 6. b 7. a 8. c 9. a 10. c

20 1. a 2. c 3. b 4. b 5. c 6. a 7. b 8. a 9. b 10. a

21 1. b 2. a 3. a 4. c 5. b 6. b 7. b 8. c 9. b 10. a

22 1. c 2. a 3. b 4. c 5. b 6. a 7. a 8. a 9. b 10. c

23 1. c 2. b 3. a 4. a 5. b 6. a 7. a 8. b 9. b 10. b

24 1. c 2. a 3. b 4. c 5. a 6. a 7. b 8. a 9. c 10. b

25 1. a 2. b 3. c 4. c 5. b 6. a 7. b 8. a 9. c 10. a

26	1. b	2. c	3. c	4. a	5. b	6. c	7. a	8. a	9. c	10. c
27	1. b	2. c	3. a	4. c	5. b	6. a	7. b	8. c	9. c	10. a
28	1. c	2. c	3. b	4. a	5. a	6. b	7. c	8. a	9. b	10. a
29	1. a	2. a	3. c	4. a	5. c	6. b	7. b	8. b	9. c	10. b
30	1. c	2. a	3. b	4. a	5. a	6. b	7. c	8. c	9. a	10. b
31	1. a	2. c	3. a	4. b	5. c	6. b	7. a	8. b	9. b	10. a
32	1. a	2. a	3. b	4. c	5. c	6. c	7. a	8. b	9. a	10. c
33	1. a	2. c	3. b	4. c	5. a	6. c	7. b	8. a	9. a	10. b
34	1. b	2. a	3. b	4. c	5. c	6. b	7. a	8. b	9. c	10. b
35	1. c	2. b	3. a	4. a	5. a	6. c	7. c	8. a	9. b	10. a
36	1. a	2. b	3. c	4. b	5. b	6. a	7. c	8. c	9. b	10. a
37	1. c	2. a	3. c	4. b	5. a	6. a	7. a	8. b	9. a	10. c
38	1. b	2. c	3. a	4. a	5. a	6. c	7. b	8. a	9. a	10. b
39	1. b	2. a	3. b	4. a	5. b	6. b	7. a	8. c	9. a	10. c
40	1. a	2. c	3. c	4. c	5. b	6. a	7. c	8. a	9. a	10. b
41	1. a	2. b	3. b	4. c	5. c	6. b	7. c	8. a	9. a	10. b
42	1. b	2. b	3. b	4. c	5. a	6. a	7. a	8. b	9. a	10. b
43	1. c	2. c	3. a	4. b	5. c	6. c	7. c	8. a	9. b	10. a
44	1. c	2. b	3. c	4. a	5. b	6. a	7. c	8. b	9. a	10. c
45	1. b	2. a	3. c	4. a	5. b	6. a	7. c	8. b	9. b	10. b
46	1. c	2. a	3. a	4. b	5. b	6. a	7. a	8. c	9. b	10. c
47	1. b	2. a	3. c	4. b	5. c	6. a	7. b	8. b	9. a	10. c
48	1. b	2. c	3. b	4. b	5. c	6. c	7. a	8. b	9. b	10. c
49	1. b	2. a	3. a	4. c	5. a	6. a	7. b	8. c	9. b	10. a
50	1. c	2. a	3. b	4. b	5. a	6. c	7. c	8. b	9. b	10. a

Progress Graph (1–25)

Directions: Write your comprehension score in the box under the selection number. Then put an x on the line above each box to show your reading time and words-per-minute reading rate.

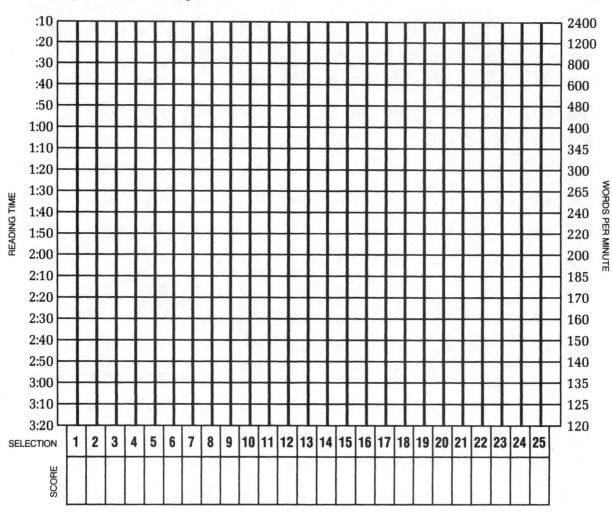

READING TIME		WORDS PER MINUTE
:10		2400
:20		1200
:30		800
:40		600
:50		480
1:00		400
1:10		345
1:20		300
1:30		265
1:40		240
1:50		220
2:00		200
2:10		185
2:20		170
2:30		160
2:40		150
2:50		140
3:00		135
3:10		125
3:20		120

SELECTION: 1 2 3 4 5 6 7 8 9 10 11 12 13 14 15 16 17 18 19 20 21 22 23 24 25

SCORE

Progress Graph (26–50)

Directions: Write your comprehension score in the box under the selection number. Then put an x on the line above each box to show your reading time and words-per-minute reading rate.

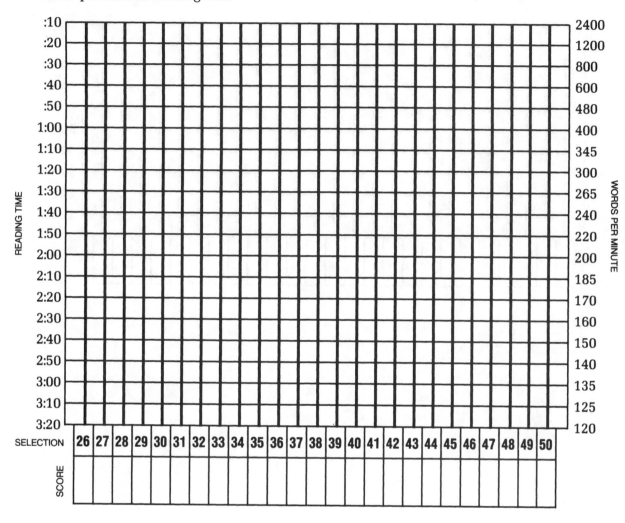

Pacing Graph

Directions: In the boxes labeled "Pace" along the bottom of the graph, write your words-per-minute rate. On the vertical line above each box, put an x to indicate your comprehension score.

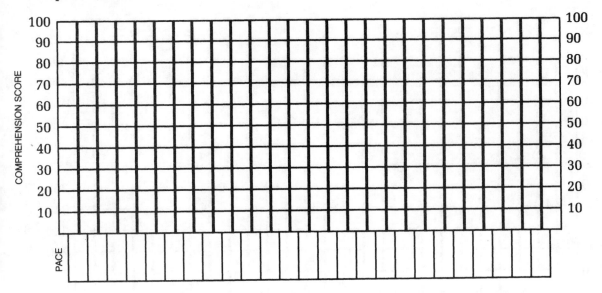